LAST
RIGHTS

BY MARYA MANNES

LAST RIGHTS
OUT OF MY TIME
THEY
BUT WILL IT SELL?
THE NEW YORK I KNOW
MORE IN ANGER
MESSAGE FROM A STRANGER

  with Norman Sheresky
UNCOUPLING

  with Robert Osborn
SUBVERSE: RHYMES FOR OUR TIMES

LAST RIGHTS

by Marya Mannes

WILLIAM MORROW & COMPANY, INC.
NEW YORK
1974

Grateful acknowledgment is made to Atheneum Publishers for permission to reprint the poem "Finally" from *The Moving Target* by W. S. Merwin, Copyright © 1963 by W. S. Merwin.

Book design by Helen Roberts

Printed in the United States of America.

2 3 4 5 77 76 75 74

Library of Congress Cataloging in Publication Data

Mannes, Marya.
    Last rights.

    Bibliography: p.
    1. Euthanasia.   2. Suicide.   I. Title.
    [DNLM: 1. Ethics, Medical.   2. Euthanasia.
    W50 M282L 1974]
    R726.M3   174'.24   73-9881
    ISBN 0-688-00211-0

Preface

As one who approached this subject with fear, who had, in the process of understanding death, to see the dying and those waiting to die, who has heard all the medical, religious, and legal arguments designed to forbid them the dignity and responsibility of their final rights, the determination to help bring these to all has become a positive and buoyant force.

That this was not a unique reaction became clear to me when I read this passage by the distinguished French historian Alfred Fabre-Luce from *La Mort a Changé*:

> *In writing this book, I seemed to relive the old myth of the Sphinx: "Find the answer or be devoured." Death says this to each of us. . . . I thought that man would have to try to transform death in order to understand it. That is, to separate from death all that reflected our own ignorance and our own weakness. The consciousness of having contributed, however slightly, to this*

humanization of the inhuman would sustain me,
I was sure, when I myself would die, however
stupidly, the death of our epoch. . . .
It is only in penetrating this profound and ter-
rible abyss that we can accept in full conscience
an attitude of hope which is of necessity ours.
Death can contradict it without triumphing
over it.

Contradiction and triumph: this is what this book is all about.

Contents

LAST
RIGHTS

I
Soundtrack

Scene: Beauty salon; woman under dryer talking to manicurist: "Well, you know, my mother started forgetting everything, so we put her away. . . . Of course, Harry and I see her every month, but I don't think she knows who we are. . . . Yeah, it's awful, she just shakes and stares."

———

Scene: Living room; two women in their sixties:
FIRST: "I have a horrible dread of being physically or mentally a defective. . . . Not able to do anything for myself; a vegetable. . . ."
SECOND: "So have I. Maybe we could make some sort of pact so that either of us could give the other a way out if we got like that. . . ."

———

Scene: A bus; young woman talking to a man:
"I went to the hospital yesterday to see my father. He's eighty, you know, with terminal cancer, and stuck full of tubes. Of course, he couldn't speak or move, but his eyes . . . Oh, God! . . . No, I don't know how long, the doctor wouldn't say."

———

Scene: Living room; a woman, her sister, her teen-age daughter:
SISTER: "Has the doctor told him yet?"
WOMAN: "Heavens, no. God knows what it would do to him."
DAUGHTER: "Told Daddy what?"
WOMAN: "Oh, nothing, dear, just something about changing nurses. Look, don't you have a test tomorrow? It's nearly nine and you . . ."
DAUGHTER (leaving): "Okay, okay. . . ."
SISTER: "Nice to see you, dear! Good luck tomorrow!"
WOMAN (lowering her voice): "I asked the nurse how bad she thought it was, but she said the doctor hadn't said anything special to her, and 'didn't Harry look much better today?' Oh God, he looks awful . . . just skin and bones, and those eyes . . ."
SISTER: "Do you think he knows?"
WOMAN: "Why should he, Gracie? He makes corny jokes, you know, to stop me worrying. He even had cereal."
SISTER: "If he knows, it must be awful."

Received, among similar thousands of letters by euthanasia organizations here and in England:

> *My own dear wife is 76 years of age and recently . . . suffered a severe stroke, resulting in partial paralysis, loss of speech. She is unable to swallow any solid foods and has difficulty swallowing liquids. Partial loss of memory and the failure of other body organs which usually accompany a severe stroke. It's breaking my heart even to watch her. . . .*

Letter from an R.N. to a California newspaper:

> *Sir: I am writing this to you hoping that all doctors and nurses may hear my plea and relieve me and my dear family of unnecessary prolonged anxiety someday when I have received my call from the great beyond, for I have no fear when that time comes, but the worry of unnecessary delay. . . . Let my fellowmen grant to me the respect of leaving this dear life for one better, with dignity, and don't punch me with unnecessary needles, someone else's dear blood, and massage and stimulate my dear old tired heart, for, dear doctor and nurse, I want very much to go in peace and be with Thee. . . . Don't use any heroic actions causing me delay, since I am at peace and have prepared many, many years ago for the time of my departure.*

Something is missing in this sound track: the voices are those of the supporting cast, not the leading players. The voices of the dying are mute: forced into silence by fear and helplessness and isolation; or by the physical incapacity to communicate. Forced by us, or—if you will—by our society in its common evasion of death.

Only a few break silence, as this woman did:

> . . . *For over three years now I have been the victim of an inoperable cancer, and have suffered greatly. It is my sincere conviction that all this prolonged suffering is quite pointless, and that persons like myself who have no possible future and face a long and painful end should be permitted by society to decide just how much more they are prepared to bear, and how long.*

And only a few who have been in the presence of death are in a position to communicate the experience to a wide public. Last year in *Newsweek*, Stewart Alsop wrote his second column on the effects of his serious, and often fatal, bone-marrow disease:

> *Oddly enough, it hasn't been as bad as it sounds. There have been some moments of fear, and some pain (a marrow test is no fun). There have been a few times when I felt very sick, and when my blood was so thin as to put my life at risk. But when you feel sick enough, you don't much fear death, and even half-welcome it. In such ways, God tempers the wind to the shorn lamb.*

God may temper the wind for the brave and the devout. But to most of us, the dread of death is such that we go to any lengths to avoid it ourselves or postpone it indefinitely in others.

In our long and obsessive passion for youth, we have —more than any other modern society—avoided direct approach to age and to dying by denying them in word, in fact, and—above all—in worth. Like Sex, until the last three decades, Death has been unmentionable in what was known as "polite society." We "pass away," not die. We do not tell our children about dying.

"Where did Uncle Ted go?" "He went to some happier place, dear." Or "He has joined his loved ones."

By barring children under sixteen from most hospitals, terminal wards, and often funerals, we shield them from the last look at the face of death and suffering, or even visits to those, young or old, who are chronically ill.

We call the old "senior citizens" or "golden-agers," and, not solely for reasons of expedience, consign them to single furnished rooms with a TV and hot plate, too often in a decaying welfare hotel, or to nursing homes which, good or bad, are anterooms to a fruitless life or a lingering lonely death.

If we keep them with us, the first sign of a faltering step or flickering mind, of a bedpan or crutch or wheelchair, spells the start of exile. They need not be old or dying to become a "burden," however cherished by the family. They can be the sick and afflicted of any age. Yet the arguments against keeping them home are reasoned and manifold:

No space at home.

Need professional care.

Bad for the children.

Tough on the family, emotionally and financially.

Better for them.

The unspoken reasons seem just as valid:

Poor dears (we say of the old), what else can we do? We are too busy with our own survival, let alone theirs.

So what most of us do to expiate our nagging guilt at leaving our ailing kin to the care of others is to give them "the best doctors have to offer," and to postpone, like the doctors, their death by any means possible. If the question of whether our loved ones *want* these means or not arises, the answer is simple: they just don't know what they want. They're too "confused" or too feeble to control their own destiny, so why ask them?

The seriously ill or the actually dying think a lot about death, but neither family nor doctors speak to them about it. They turn it away with a smiling "Nonsense!", or "Back on your feet in no time," or "You're looking just fine!"

Death is a dirty word, and because they know it the doomed themselves often try to deny it, pushing it under the rug of rejection—hidden. The unspoken word is itself an isolation ward.

Because of this there are none lonelier than the stricken and chronically ill of any age. They cannot speak of what concerns them most.

Yet their isolation may slowly be coming to an end. The chorus of voices who speak for them and for their final rights is swelling steadily, if not yet victoriously, above the discordant oratorio of church and state, of medicine and law.

The name of the oratorio is euthanasia, and its first notes were sounded many centuries ago in the language that named it, Greek. Meaning: "a good, or peaceful, death."

And Socrates, who chose to drink hemlock rather than be slain for his heresies, said, "Death may be the greatest of all human blessings."

Two thousand years later, the chorus goes on:

> . . . *My mother was 88 and deaf and blind. She suffered a lesion of the brain in June and quickly became bed-ridden. Pneumonia was expected to carry her off but huge quantities of drugs prevented this, causing her to linger on in a pitiful physical condition and mental tor-*

ment. . . . It made me afraid to go on living
knowing that anything so terrible could happen
at the end of one's life. . . .

The most hideous aspect of it all was that I
actually wondered whether she was exhibiting
signs of drug addiction. . . . she had frequent
spells of incessant talking. . . . she had delu-
sions. . . . she kept saying she was going mad
and repeatedly asked for "my pill." . . .

A change in the law cannot come soon enough
to prevent such prolonging of the act of dying.
. . . The dead themselves would be its strong-
est supporters.

Perhaps. But the living supporters of "a good death"
are speaking in greater and greater numbers for the
dying and for those who love them, tend them, and
minister to them.

The chorus is swelling now because two things have
happened within the last decades that demand a profound change in our whole attitude toward death:
individual, social, and moral. One is the advanced technology that permits doctors to prolong life beyond its
long-accepted limits. The other is the ever-increasing
fight of the individual to maintain and exercise his
rights over matters affecting his life and death, his mind
and his body.

Religious faith may ease the passage for those who
believe in the justice of a Supreme Being and an immortality denied all other organisms on earth.

The concept of immortality or transfiguration is still
a profound force in eastern religions and in some primitive societies.

But for most of us in the increasingly secular nations
of the West, such comforts and promises are hard to
sustain. Against what inner longings and hopes still

linger, death still seems final and irreversible: the end of self, the beginning of nothing.

Whether it is indeed the "beginning of nothing" we do not know, since death in terms of the spirit remains a mystery. A Swedish doctor, weighing terminal patients on an extremely sensitive scale and noting a small weight loss at the moment of death, claims to have uncovered a quantitative measure—if not proof of existence—of the soul. It weighs twenty-one grams. The weight of a sigh, perhaps? Of sorrow or relief?

What is no mystery is our common fear: of dying. if not of death. We should know too that fear has always been a diminisher of life. Whether bred in the bogs of superstition or clothed in the brocades of dogma and ritual, the specter of death has reduced the living to supplicants, powerless.

Awe in itself can be an enlargement, whether felt at the birth of a child or for magnificent music or at the incandescent flight of men to the moon. Yet awe, compounded by dread and fear, has been a consistent block to the development of the human spirit and a humane society.

It is this block that the acceptance and practice of euthanasia must—and will—dissolve. The right to choose death when life no longer holds meaning is not only the next liberation but the last human right.

The great creative beings of history have known this, and their voices will be heard in these pages as summonses to courage in the face of death: from Seneca to Shakespeare, from Socrates to Einstein, from Emily Dickinson to Walt Whitman, who wrote:

Dark Mother always gliding near with soft feet,
Have none chanted for thee a chant of fullest welcome?
Then I chant it for thee; I glorify thee above all:

I bring thee a song, that when thou must indeed come,
Come unfalteringly.

Yet within this orchestra of death, the arbiters of our social and physical patterns play strongly in counterpoint.

A lawyer, to a layman: "The minute you have a law permitting or assisting the death of another—however benign in purpose—you open a can of worms. Remember Hitler's 'experiments'? What makes you think it could never happen here?"

A priest: "The Lord giveth, the Lord taketh away. Even a merciful doctor cannot play God."

A distinguished surgeon: "Yes, I have pulled out the life supports when I was convinced the patient had no conceivable chance of recovery—let's say, irretrievably comatose. A lot of us do. But in most cases, life is paramount. You never know the extent of the patient's will to live, you've got to respect that and help it. It can work miracles. So can new treatments."

An internist at a major hospital who is also a Protestant minister: "I am a Vitalist—that is, I believe in the divinity of human life, period. The *fact* of life, of living, is the main concern. People who believe that the *quality* of life is what counts more—well, that's an upper-class concept."

Yet the physician cannot afford the luxury of concepts. His and his alone are the final decisions. Surrounded as he is, in intensive-care units, by his technical team, he alone is the arbiter, guardian of his patients —whether victims of accident, cancer, cardiac failure, chronic affliction, or failing life-forces. Relatives can and do plead with him to "do all you can" or, in terminal cases "please don't do anything." Most are committed to the first, many silently concur with the second in cases of massive damage to vital organs or the relentless ebbing of life in the helpless old.

When the young or the middle-aged suffer serious illness, time, will, and a resistant body work in their favor. Especially time. New therapies, new drugs, new machines, new transplant techniques may not only allow remissions of their disease but often return them to a productive life.

The old and stricken can hope for such miracles but seldom wait for them. They can only long for peace from pain—and wait for death.

In waiting rooms.

II
Pictures

The heart asks pleasure first,
And then, excuse from pain;
And then, those little anodynes
That deaden suffering;

And then, to go to sleep;
And then, if it should be
The will of its Inquisitor,
The liberty to die.

Emily Dickinson

THE WAITING ROOMS

Scene: In one of the prestigious suburbs of a midwestern city, across the road from its big hospital, the grassy compound with low brick buildings, quasi-colonial, hardly looks like a nursing home. Only the impeccable lawns and the clean-edged pebble drives suggest "institution" rather than community. We see plenty of cars in the parking lot but very few people. There is a curious emptiness, a mute suspension.

Once inside the main long building we can see why. There is an office in the entrance, and opposite it a very large visiting room that suggests the nature of this top-grade home. A sterile muteness, again: of impersonal decoration in genteel shades, of total order. It is a place to sit in but not to use.

As the big fat cheery nurse in white, who came to greet us and show us around, often said, "We try to make it as much like home as we can. They can see visitors here, and of course there's a television set in the corner there. . . ."

The long corridors were immaculate. She gave us glimpses of private and double rooms, and some with four, most with old women lying on the beds, few moving. The rooms were spacious and bright, and though most had television, no set was turned on.

We were shown a huge kitchen, so shiningly modern, so flawlessly ordered, that it might have been a laboratory in an outer-space movie. We also saw rooms equipped with devices that could ease a sitting patient down into a bath, or hoist one, in a canvas sling, into a shower. There, too, were gleaming new-model wheelchairs that patients, restrained in them by a table-tray ("so they won't *feel* restrained"), could operate themselves.

"We potty them every two hours," said the nurse, "if you'll excuse the expression!" and added that it "sort of reminded them of when they were babies" and they got used to it.

There was a room for hairdressing, "good for morale!" and of course a big dining room. "We encourage them to eat here instead of in their own rooms; you know, to socialize. They have bingo nights here, and sort of holiday gatherings. And if they can't hold cards, we have volunteer staff to hold cards for them."

How many patients could they take care of? "About sixty-eight," said the nurse. And when we noted the seeming absence of men, she said well, yes, there were only seven or eight, but (sighing) "they die younger, of course."

"Do your patients ever speak about death or dying?"

Cheerily, "Oh, yes, some of them. But you know, like one of them said just yesterday, 'I want to die,' and then right away, 'Can I have two eggs?'"

We asked her whether in terminal cases they were ever helped to die.

Shocked, she said, "Oh, no, that's God's will. *He* decides."

What about giving them sedation when they asked for it?

Shocked again, she said sternly, "We never give them anything without doctors' orders. That's the law, you know. The doctors decide everything."

We nodded our understanding and walked back through corridors empty of people to the entrance hall. It was early afternoon and the patients might have been napping, but the lack of movement and sound (not even murmurs or chatter from the rooms) was disquieting. The place seemed "ideal," and we told the nurse so. But we left equipped with brochure and price list (in case a fabricated "old cousin" applied for admission), and with deep depression.

It costs a thousand or more a month to stay in this home. A private room is fifty-one dollars a day; a semi-private thirty-nine dollars a day. All medical services, from drugs to physiotherapy to cleaners, are extra. Clearly only wealthy patients or those with rich relatives could afford it, and the nurse had reeled off a list of prominent and powerful people who had come, or sent their loved ones, to this superior place—"dedicated," the brochure read, "to the Restoration of Health . . . and the Renewal of Spirit."

"Even if I could afford it," said the putative cousin of the putative aging relative, "I'd rather put a bullet through my head."

———

Scene: A nursing home in a small rural northeastern community. Formerly the home of a prosperous local resident, it was built of white clapboard, fronted by a small porch, surrounded by lawns and trees.

We passed a porch where six very old men and women were sitting.

They were looking straight ahead, at nothing. They did not speak to each other.

We were led by a nurse to Ada's room. It was large enough for three beds, quite close together. Ada's bed, rails up, was in the corner. The other two flanked a window.

In one lay a woman, stretched on her back in a stiff line, her gray-haired head, propped on pillows, facing straight ahead. Her face, well-fleshed and ruddy, never changed expression. It was a curious combination of humor and contempt; unsettling. In the other bed a very old woman, face turned away and scarcely visible, lay feet curled up. Her eyes were open, facing the wall. She never spoke.

A friend who apparently knew her well was visiting Ada: a thin little woman with sparse white hair drawn back from her small-boned narrow face. Her feet, in socks, stuck through the bars, her shaking skeletal hands clutched the rail as she responded to her visitor in a German-accented voice.

During the twenty bedside minutes, her mind shifted back and forth in time and space.

"And you know, he likes *preiselbeeren* and sauerbraten so much, so I cook him that," she said of her husband, now ten years dead. Her granddaughter is her daughter; she asks her old friend who she is; she asks, "What is this holiday today?" when there is none. She has long since forgotten what day, what year, she is in.

But not what place she came from: Halle. We speak to her in German, and she tells us where Halle is, and suddenly the drifting mists lift for a moment and she speaks of origins.

Then she says, "You don't have to speak German. I know English," with a glance of mild reproof.

And she knows, too, where she is. She says, "They never come, why don't they come?" and you think she is speaking of the attendants, but after a silence she says, with anger, "They should come with the car and take me home, where is the car?"

Her friend asks, "Do you want anything, Ada—something to eat or drink?"

Clutching the bed rail, shaking a little, Ada says, clearly, "Yes, I want something, I want to get out of here, I want my freedom!"

Then she subsides, her eyelids turn down. Her friend pats her, nods to me as she says, "I know what you want, dear. You want some Thunderbird. We'll get you your Thunderbird!"

"*Ja!*" says Ada. We go to the pantry and ask the nice woman for Ada's bottle. "Not much left," she says, and brings a quarter-full bottle of the cheap wine out of the refrigerator. "Don't give her much," she says, pouring an inch of it into a paper cup.

Her friend says, "She loves this stuff," as she carries it to her bedside and, slowly and carefully, transfers the cup into Ada's trembling eager hands, half-holding it for her because the cup tips precariously.

Sipping slowly, Ada's face brightens. She drinks like a child or a bird at the basin. But when she is finished and the cup taken gently from her, the mists close in.

The friend turns her head to address the motionless woman sitting up in the opposite bed. "Do you like visitors?" she asks.

"Not particularly," she says, implacable.

"Tell Bobby I make him sauerbraten tonight," Ada says to her old friend. Then, "Who are you?" and finally, "When will they come?"

Ada's family pays six hundred dollars a month to keep her there. They visit her once a week for twenty minutes.

———————

Scene: A run-down area of a northern city. In what used to be an "elegant" part of town, there is a row of handsome ornate mansions built in the nineteen hundreds for people with money, fame, or large families. Five stories high, with cornices, stoops, balustrades, and window adornments, they were built also for long life.

But for the last fifty years few could afford them for private living: what staff would climb the stairs, for what burgeoning sums? So for some time now they have become nursing homes for the old.

In the hot summer days you can see them, men and

women, huddled on benches and chairs on the small front stoop, for air, for sun, for change. Some of the homes have what they call "terraces" in back, but they aren't much larger, nor less crowded with the bemused, ailing, and motionless old.

Inside, these nursing homes vary widely in atmosphere, care, and management, if not in cost. One of the worst of them, in fact, charges $200 a week for keeping its charges in rooms with four beds while another offers private care for $180 a week.

"Offers" is hardly the word. The waiting lists are months behind and hundreds long, and only the house staff or the social agencies of the city know when a vacancy opens for a new referral. As one supervisor said tartly, "Y'know, they keep on living, they just cling on. . . ." (as if this were a nuisance, like incontinence).

So what do these "lingerers"—black, white, Puerto Rican, most on Social Security and Medicaid—get for over $9,800 a year (excluding doctors' fees)?

In the better houses on this row, care and cleanliness were self-evident; and bright wallpapers, scrubbed floors, and a pleasant staff helped to ameliorate—for the patient if not the observer—a condition of nonbeing hard to accept for any sentient human.

But who knows how sentient are the prisoners of time, the very old sitting in wheelchairs, lying cramped and sideways in their beds, or ringed about the table of the "social" room? Very few of them talk, or look specifically at anything, even the TV set. Animation may set in when (if) their families visit them, but all they are really doing is waiting. "Cling on." To what?

Entering one of the homes on this street (to explore the care possibilities for a nonexistent older sister with a broken hip and a wandering mind) the lobby seemed to lack the usual office and was pervaded instead by that mixture of disinfectant and unaired flesh that marks failing functions.

A very assured, very tough, and very mod young black woman asked our business: sharply, and with evident reluctance to show us the rest of the establishment. It was a bad time, she was busy, all the floors were alike, and anyway the waiting list was forever, and what agency referred us to them? We said, none, this was a preliminary look for possibilities should this sister be moved from her present home with friends in the suburbs to New York, where we could see her more regularly.

She finally showed us a small room with four beds and one window on the street and took us to one of several "social rooms." It was empty, dingy, and stuffy, with a jar of crushed red paper flowers in the middle of the table and crumbs on the floor.

No, they had no terrace. If patients wanted to go out in good weather, their relatives could take them in cars.

It was abundantly clear that at two hundred dollars a week her patients were at best an intrusion, at worst a burden; and that we, too, wasted her (well-paid) time.

At still another, halfway between the best and the worst, we passed a middle-aged man addressed by a nurse as "Doctor." Stooped, gray-haired, his waxen face in folds of failure, he seemed one very small step from those he was treating.

For what? he must ask himself every day, every hour. For what?

And what happens when the inmates of these waiting rooms are really sick? Back to the hospital, of course. "We can't handle 'em here."

THE MACHINES

All intensive-care units have the same elements: the prone bodies on the beds; the machines to which they are attached; the upright or bending bodies of the doctors and their teams.

Take three particular patients in the intensive-care unit of a great city hospital: one woman with cancer of the kidney, her young face motionless, eyes closed; one white-haired woman with a brain tumor, twitching her head back and forth, side to side; and one middle-aged man with an acute coronary.

All were bound by rubber or plastic tubing from nose or mouth or temple or wrist or abdomen or leg to hanging liquids or to wall-hung machines that monitored the beat, in fine Spencerian oscillations, of heart and lung and blood and brain. EKG (electrocardiogram) for the heart, EEG (electroencephalograph) for the brain, and a Bennett MA-1 respirator that breathes for them.

If you ask what certain other gadgets are, you will be told that a brilliant surgeon developed not long ago a technique of "total parenteral nutrition" which makes it possible to feed patients by catheterizing a large vein and giving them glucose, fats, amino acids, and vitamins. They need a big vein for that so that irritating amino acids can be well diluted. You drip it in all day long, a little at a time.

There's also something called an arterial transducer—a sensor—attached usually to the calf of the leg so that peripheral arterial pressure can insure that blood is getting to the toes, or whatever, so they won't develop gangrene.

One is also told that this kind of support is the same whether the patient was in terminal pneumonitis from Bleomycin toxicity, or had a cerebral vascular accident, etc.

Are all these three terminal, one asks? "We never really know," says the doctor. "Sometimes they surprise you."

What about the woman who's thrashing about so? "Oh, she's having hallucinations. Delirious. But she's not in pain."

Oh.

No one will tell you how long they will last . . . a week, a month, maybe much longer. Clearly, the patient doesn't know. Nor the doctor.

The EKG moves in peaks, so the brain is alive. When it's just a flat line, the brain's dead. But what does the moving finger record when it isn't flat? Thought processes? Dreams? Will? Desire? Nothing?

Is this consciousness? Medically perhaps. Humanly?

What to medical men is a miracle of science, a brilliant tool, a guardian of life, a redeemer of death may be all these things. To the lay eye, it seems a vast entrapment, not unlike the moth caught in the spider's net and wrapped and wrapped in a shroud of filaments till the spider can feast on it quietly, at its ease.

Morbid, of course; an emotional reaction to think of these bodies on beds as imprisoned, as Gullivers bound by a race of pygmies. When in reality, the doctors are the giants, performing the impossible with the aid of machines on your father, your son, your mother, your sister . . . yourself?

You would not know, because presumably you would not be thinking or knowing or feeling. You will either go out when the little fingers cease their writing, or you will awake one day and crawl back slowly into consciousness and another day—and another day—to live. What life? No one but yourself can tell you that. Or for how long.

But according to what we have been taught, anything is better than nothing. Even for those who must live with a machine for want of a kidney, or with someone else's heart, and at the overwhelming and usually ruinous expense of those who must pay for either.

An intern rolls in a new patient, another makes the rounds of the machines, checking the charts.

Intensive-care units are no place for strangers. They are the twilight zones between life and death, the ultimate laboratories of the mad scientists and the sane revivers, who have learned to save nearly everything but the human soul.

How can one plug in, then, to what none can define? And to what?

III
The Doctors

1.

"I have now been told that I've got cancer. The thought of death has never worried me. But the manner of going has.

"I'm not a brave person, nor a shining one, the thoughts of what I've before me is making every moment a hell for me. I could enjoy what is left for me if I knew I'd be given euthanasia as soon as my time came. My dog shall have the best of a peaceful death. Why not me?" So writes a woman.

The doctor knows why not. He is committed by oath and by instinct to preserve life, to help live if not heal. And the incredible new medical technology has made it possible for highly disciplined teams of surgeons—cardiologists, neurologists, lung, liver, bone, and tissue specialists—to keep stricken organisms alive even if the brain is irretrievably damaged or lung and heart incapable of functioning without mechanical help. Now it is not dust to dust, but human to vegetable.

22

So the woman who wrote the letter asking "Why not?" will probably end in a hospital ward; bound by a race of technicians to the hanging life fluids of blood and oxygen and to the electric signals of her brain and heart and liver and marrow.

The pain that first signaled and then invaded her whole organism will be dulled periodically by potent drugs, time-tested and new, and she may have the euphoric moments that herald addiction.

The doctors know she is terminal, and an increasing minority face this knowledge squarely and compassionately by removing the life supports of an organism that only the new machines record as "living." They are not always happy about this. Not only is it still a risk, in many communities in this country, for a doctor to make even this negative gesture in the name of mercy, but it can still court malpractice suits, suspension of license, and official censure. Even without these hazards, it goes against every grain in his long conditioning as a saver of life.

He could even view it as an admission of failure. The death of a patient is the defeat of the healer. Even though his patients are palpably dying, he cannot say, "Let my people go!" So he is bound, like his dying charge, by a network of professional conscience, technical miracles, an accusing society, pleading relatives, and critical colleagues that tend to inhibit his simple humanity. Moreover, if he can add even a week, a month, six months of life to his patient, however tormented or senseless they may be, he has done his best.

At a Senate Special Committee on Aging last year, Dr. Warren T. Reich, a senior researcher at the Kennedy Center of Bioethics in Washington, said that, "The terminal patient may desperately want rest, peace and dignity, yet he may receive only infusions, transfusions, a machine and a team of experts busily occupied with his pulmonary functions but not with him as a person."

Eric Hodgins, a former editor of *Fortune* Magazine, author and productive survivor of a serious stroke, would heartily agree with him. "Well, I do not think I want a team at my last bedside, whatever its previous diagnostic value may have been. I just want an individual who is understanding and compassionate: who will never confuse the prolongation of life with the prolongation of death. . . .

"In today's cold society the recipient of extensive medical care is bound increasingly to wonder, 'How many more advances in medicine can I stand?' For he feels with full intensity the force of a miserable paradox: the paradox of advancing medicine and deteriorating patient care."

Many, both in and out of the medical profession, would claim that patient care was never more advanced and comprehensive than now. But Hodgins was clearly talking in human, not technical, terms. And those of us fortunate enough to have had a trusted "family doctor" remember that he came to know us as intimately as kin or close friend. Aware not only of his patient's medical history but of his intrinsic humanity as an individual, the good general practitioner was also confessor and confidant.

Some doctors still try to be all these now, though the demands on their time and specific skills are so great that the physician-to-patient talk-in-depth becomes curtailed and rare.

It becomes increasingly rare as the patient's life span draws to its close. Even when a doctor knows his patient is terminal, he will preserve the illusion of hope and ongoing life not only by exhaustive medical means but by withholding the truth from the patient if not the relatives.

PATIENT: Doctor, how sick *am* I? The pain seems worse and worse!

DOCTOR: We're doing all we can to relieve that . . . it's a cyclic condition. I'll tell the nurse to increase your dosage today. . . .

PATIENT: Yes, but what *is* it? Is there any *real* cure?

DOCTOR: (*patting her gently on the shoulder*) A lot of it's up to you. Think positive, Mrs. Blair! (*He leaves her bed with a smile and a wave.*)

HUSBAND OF PATIENT: Doctor, how far has this spread? Has she any real chance?

DOCTOR: We're doing everything to see that she has.

HUSBAND: Yes, but it's spreading, isn't it?

DOCTOR: Tell me, Mr. Blair, have you told her it's cancer?

HUSBAND: No, but I think she knows. She keeps asking me. . . .

DOCTOR: Well, there's no point in rousing her fears. If she keeps asking, when we give her radiation, just say it's local, or something like that. It's very important to keep up her morale.

Doctors are human beings. It is sometimes hard to remember this because of their exalted position. They are exalted because they know more about the body than its inhabitor does. And since we cannot function without our bodies, our lives are wholly in the hands of our physicians, at their mercy, and for their disposition.

As human beings, doctors are individuals, differing one from another in personality and manner. But their superior status, their common power, produce common attitudes reinforced by a society and its media that—perhaps more than any other—tends to deify them. The doctor's shining armor is his white coat. He is the healer and savior, performing his tender miracles behind closed doors while anguished or hopeful lovers and relatives wait outside for his verdict of life or death.

In real life, his looks are secondary. His attitudes are not. The medical profession is by and large a conservative one, if only because its sworn duty is to conserve life. New inventions and techniques, proven to be assets, it welcomes. New ideas it greets with skepticism, especially if they emanate from outside the close medical circle.

Recent studies and surveys provide factual evidence that medical students and physicians fear death more than do other professional groups. It seems entirely logical that the strong drive impelling them toward the goal of preserving life should stem in part, at least, from aversion to death itself. As one who has seen a color film showing autopsies of cadavers, the long incisions opening on the diseased and bloody matter that was once miracle, I can understand why early training in dissection could foster this aversion.

To a surgeon so oriented against death and toward action to prevent it, a dying patient can become a threat to his own mastery of the situation.

Ironically, the new technological team that supports the doctor prolonging life can benefit the doctor more than the patient. It provides not only a diversion from this threat, but a welcome distraction from the person-to-person confrontation of doctor-to-patient that the gravely ill or dying crave.

Nobody knows about this need more than Dr. Elisabeth Kübler-Ross, a Swiss-born psychiatrist whose book *On Death and Dying* was the end result of hundreds of confrontations with the terminally ill.

She herself originated and conducted these interdisciplinary seminars in the late sixties as assistant professor of psychiatry at the University of Chicago and assistant director of the Psychiatric Consultation and Liaison Service of the University of Chicago hospitals. Joining her in these were students of medicine, sociology, psychology, and theology. When they first made their rounds to the various hospitals, the reactions of several administrators ranged from annoyance to outright refusal to cooperate. Outsiders talking to *their* patients, disrupting *their* routines, usurping *their* functions? As time went on, however, Dr. Ross and her seminars were found to be not only of visible support to those in the last stages of illness, but of real impact on medical philosophy.

In this extraordinary free exchange, the terminal patients for once became central figures, were given the dignity of worth and recognition in a society that often denied them both. Their interlocutors, in turn, learned more from the dying than their family or professional experience had ever taught them.

What emerged from long video-taped interviews with about five hundred patients was the fact that most of them went through five different stages on their *via crucis* to death.

The first was denial. "No, not me." Neither they, nor often their families, could accept the fatal prognosis.

Denial then turned very quickly to anger. The patient was resentful, hard to handle, extremely demanding, and largely uncooperative. The natural reaction of the staff was, understandably if unfortunately, to make their visits infrequent, to treat them harshly, like intractable children, and to worsen their sense of isolation.

Dr. Ross called the third stage "bargaining"—for more time, for special favors in return for better behavior, for reassurance instead of acceptance.

When this pitiful game is abandoned, a slough of depression sets in, turning the patients inward toward deep remembered losses and away even from their loved ones. The worst that those close to the patient can then do is to tell them to "cheer up." Grief should not only be open, but openly encouraged.

Although these stages might not follow the same sequence in each patient, or might at times coexist, it did, however, become obvious to the listening groups that the need for communication was greatest during denial of death and the final acceptance.

And since nurses have for so long been trained to be cheerful and families conditioned to avoid talk of death, the doctor who joins this plot of evasion in the name of kindness or comfort is only contributing to the deep isolation surrounding the stricken patient.

In a profession that makes biological continuance the absolute good, the price is the loss of dignity of the individual. Since doctors are only reflecting the cultural inability of their society to face death, their efforts to prolong life and relieve suffering often merely prolong the act of dying, and inflict suffering.

Not only has the study of death and dying been absent from the curriculum of high schools and colleges, whether in humanistic or biological terms, but not until very recently has it been given any emphasis in medical training. Care for the living has so far precluded studies of care for the dying, except in the techniques of sedation, resuscitation, or postponement. The surgeon can therefore hang out his shingle with full confidence that he can revive a blue baby or the victim of a car crash but without clear attitudes toward the terminally ill. He understands senility as the disease of age and as the degeneration of vital organs, but he rarely knows—except in matters of pain and its reduction—what the dying individual of any age or affliction is feeling and thinking, especially when speech is barely possible. He has, in any event, so little time to talk, and less desire.

A failure in most professions is seldom crucial. That a lawyer should lose a case, a merchant a sale, or an author a contract, may be sharp and temporary depressants. To a doctor committed to life, however, a patient's death—no matter how inevitable—is a form of failure.

New values, in any event, are slow to develop in a profession by and large conservative, suspicious of change, and deeply protective of its superior place in American society: daily enforced by an American public glued daily to the small moving images of men in white, healing the sick and maimed in immaculate hospitals staffed by lovely nurses and handsome interns while they comfort their patients or bend over anesthetized bodies; sharp eyes peering over white masks, deft hands making crucial incisions. Some doctors may have personal problems, but then who doesn't in TV serials?

If you believed these hospital dramas, you would think not only that the United States provides superb care for all citizens (no fees are mentioned, of course), that Marcus Welby, M.D., is ever ready to jump in his car and visit his patients, exuding wisdom and comfort from every compassionate pore.

Would it were so. Possibly it still is, for patients rich enough to afford private rooms at two thousand dollars a month and for the remaining handful of doctors who can afford to be Marcus Welby—family doctor, general practitioner, the man who knows and loves the people he treats and takes time to talk to them.

But until recently the profession as a whole and the American Medical Association in particular have fiercely resisted any national health plan that would at least lighten in part the intolerable burden of sickness for the poor as well as the solvent, and make health care—preventive as well as immediate—available to all Americans. The bugaboo of "socialism" has been hurled at each move toward the kind of system already functioning remarkably well in Britain and in the Scandinavian countries: a fact observable to visitors who have found themselves needing good medical care with minimal cost—and getting it. Certainly, our medical equipment is unparalleled, our research facilities and technical prowess the envy of smaller and poorer nations. But in the process, too many doctors have had to become automated, along with the diagnostic machines that are their servants.

They monitor the screens and derive their prognoses, and science can keep their patients alive—at mountainous cost—beyond any span credible in past history.

But no machine can tell them what to say to a dying patient and ease him truthfully but gently into death.

Except for this vital function, now assumed instead by psychiatrists or social workers or clergymen, doctors can perform one final act of compassion. They can pull out the life supports that keep a dying brain and body alive.

"An increasing number of us now do," said one surgeon friend, "I would guess about fifty percent at least. We don't talk about it—it's just something a lot of us feel must be done when there's no alternative."

His estimates seem modest. In a recent poll at the University of Washington, 87 percent of responding members of the Association of Professors of Medicine favored passive euthanasia—passive in the sense of removing certain mechanical life sustainers ("pulling the plug" from organs unable to exist without them)—and 80 percent said they practiced it. Only 15 percent, however, were in favor of active euthanasia: administering a drug which, although designed to relieve pain, could hasten death.

At a community hospital, researchers found that among staff physicians and first- and fourth-year medical students, 59 percent of the doctors, 69 percent of the first-year students, and 90 percent of the fourth-year students favored passive euthanasia.

These might seem comforting statistics for those dreading prolongation of existence without viable life. They suggest also a rising new breed of doctors more concerned with human dignity than with technical supremacy.

Yet the distinctions made between "active" and "passive" are conveniently tenuous in medical terms, and susceptible to wide interpretations. They also give no hint of the time lapse involved before the doctor's commission of either. He may delay his "passive" act of termination for weeks, even months, after his ebbing patient has been the helpless object of mechanical prolongation.

Who knows, in any event, whether your doctor might not be one of the 20 or 30 percent *opposed* to euthanasia, or one of the 85 percent who would not administer a pain-relieving drug likely to cause death?

Furthermore, doctors know that in legal terms euthanasia can still be equated with murder or, at the very least, with malpractice.

That such suits are relatively infrequent and that we rarely hear of them is owing to two factors: the increasing acknowledgment by the hospital staff that "pulling the plug" is widely practiced, if not always approved, and that there is a growing tendency among relatives of the dying to plead for it.

The patient's own choice, however, is not polled. It is not even solicited.

2.

The nurses who are close to the terminally ill are even closer to the doctor; by necessity not only privy to his actions but to the charts and prognoses that determine them.

Some, raised in religious doctrines, may privately equate even passive euthanasia with sin and suffer inner conflicts between their faith and their physician when he commits it. Trained to deal with the dying (but expressly not with their families), many hospital nurses still share the national aversion to talking about it when their patients most need a dialogue.

Yet here again the wall is being breached, as the subsequent interviews with nurses indicate:

———

"Don't you want some pain medicine?"
"Oh, yes."
The nurse often asks the patient if he wants something before he asks for it. "We try to anticipate pain rather than have patients beg for relief."

"Some families I see hate to see pain. But I often find it difficult to find the doctor so I can ask him to increase dosage. Some families ask for still more pain relief. They don't want to be the ones to give the lethal dose, but they will often ask for more relief. In hospitals, doctors often ask the nurses if the dosages are strong enough—for example, 'Should we go from Demerol to morphine?'

"We try to stay on top of pain, one step ahead of it all the time, so the patient doesn't have to be anxious about his pain getting worse.

"When the end is near, all doctors are pretty liberal with drugs—though they do differ, and some hold off on high dosages until the end is near."

———

"Some doctors are reluctant to move from a weaker drug to the next stronger one because they anticipate much greater pain later. So there can be a time in the middle of the terminal stage when pain is not fully relieved.

"Some doctors will write on the records—'No heroic measures.' Others will say it to the nurses but not write it.

"Incidentally, a patient's pain often decreases when he is finally told the truth of his disease and its seriousness. About fifty percent of doctors tell their patients all. An equal percentage doesn't.

"During the terminal phase, a good percentage of patients say, 'I want to go.' But they may just be testing what the nurse will do or say—particularly if they're not sure they are dying. When a patient says, 'I wish I could get it all over with,' it may be a ploy to test reactions. So it's hard to say how many patients honestly ask for death."

———

"I know of a cancer patient with a distended abdomen and paralysis from the waist down and spinal metastases. The patient developed a bad infection in the blood and the doctor later regretted using antibiotics—because it prolonged a bad life. The doctor became depressed and the nurses had to console him."

———

"You know, nurses have a lot to say about whether a seriously ill patient shall live or die. They don't *have* to call triple page [resuscitation team] when the doctor has not given instructions.

"In general, young nurses and doctors have had no contact with death—or even chronic illness. So young nurses and doctors often get very close to the patient. In fact, experienced nurses, who know enough not to get too involved, have to console younger nurses and doctors.

"I don't believe in transplants. It's too much like vultures to me."

———

"The families often give the clues of what they want you to do. A woman may say, 'You have other work to do, so don't stay here too long.' This is her way of saying, 'Let my husband die.'"

———

"Only old, old people, seventy to ninety, accept death with no fear or regret. They're tired, and death is a release.

"Yes, I've pulled the plug on doctors' orders, but never on my own initiative. Some nurses have done it on their own. Most doctors are fairly conservative and will wait it out until the last moments of life. Some doctors will pull the IV's and some won't.

"Many families don't want extreme measures. Some say, 'Why are you doing anything?' "

"I know one case of a Negro man in Cleveland who wanted to shorten his life and her suffering by shooting his wife. She was awful-looking from cancer of the uterus, she was a skeleton covered with skin. I talked him out of it, saying, 'Nature is taking its course; don't speed it up.' So I think that often the argument for euthanasia in terminal illness comes from the suffering family, not the patient. But that doesn't mean euthanasia is unjustified. I had a case of a family's using up a five weeks' supply of pills and narcotics in one day. The patient died, of course. My policy is not to blow the whistle, and I didn't."

"I think euthanasia is a bigger problem in nursing homes and rest homes. Expense is a gigantic problem for patients at almost all of these places."

[She was not exaggerating. In the big metropolitan hospitals, intensive-care units cost $155 a day, nurses $160 a day. The chronically ill in private rooms pay $122 to $132 daily; in wards, $90 to $95.

Aside from a $120 fee per hour for use of the operating rooms and machines, a surgeon's fee for open-heart surgery ranges from $2,000 to $5,000, a transplant from

$15,000 to $20,000, and a kidney operation $10,000. These costs may deviate according to type of hospital from 10 percent less or more, but are national estimates.]

———————

"I think that if a person has brain damage that is irreversible—for example, an old lady who can't feed, speak, or dress herself—then euthanasia is justified. I know I wouldn't want to die that way, though I might not even care because I wouldn't know my own condition. Anyway, we had an elderly lady like the one I just described. We called her 'crazy Mary.' She was about sixty. The husband tried to keep her at home but she was almost an animal, and he had to lock her indoors. He finally put her in a nursing home.

"There is a trend to discharge chronically ill patients to extensive-care facilities or to their own homes. This is partly because hospitals are crowded, partly because doctors and nurses don't like to deal with the dying, partly because some patients prefer to live and die at home, partly because family doctors, particularly experienced older men, have a liberal attitude about the use of painkillers [i.e., they are not afraid of giving a "lethal dosage"]. After all, who will ever know?

"Usually families who give care to dying patients have large dosages of narcotics at hand. When the patient leaves the hospital, they take one or two vials of morphine—twenty to thirty cc. per vial. We usually start the dose at one or two cc., so you can see the family has the means to give a lethal dose.

"Incidentally, the problem is beyond that of mere pain control. There may be distention, diet restrictions, dyspnea, nausea, incontinence—the loss of control and dignity. These can be more painful than physical pain.

And we can't control these problems as well as we do physical pain.

"If you want to die 'well' and be sure of freedom from heroics and antipain-killer doctors, the best thing to do is pick your doctor with care. Agree on your right to know the truth and share in decisions about care. Remember that most doctors are compassionate men. They are not sadists or ogres."

Clearly doctors are not sadists or ogres. They share the same conflicts as the families and nurses of the dying but theirs alone is the solution—not necessarily within themselves—of the life and death of their patients. In the final process, none can tell them what to say to the dying.

One physician affiliated with a great Southern California hospital said, "I always tell a man with responsibilities what his condition is and what to prepare for. I think he has the right and obligation to set his affairs in order. It's bad enough for his family if he dies, but it's worse if he leaves them in a mess."

Wise doctors can judge the capacity of a "responsible" patient, with commitments, to accept such pragmatic warnings. There is still a sharp division however, between those who are able and willing to communicate truth and those who evade it, isolating the patient in defense of themselves and "lack of time."

No matter what course is taken with the terminal patient, most doctors try to be as honest as possible with the distraught and grieving family. How the family responds is a major factor in the acceptance or rejection of euthanasia, in the torment or peace preceding the final passage.

IV
The Family

No one probed more deeply the pain of dying in an aura of deceit and isolation than Leo Tolstoy in "The Death of Ivan Ilych":

> *What tormented Ivan Ilych most was the deception, the lie, which for some reason they all accepted, that he was not dying but was simply ill, and that he only need keep quiet and undergo a treatment and then something very good would result. He however knew that do what they would nothing would come of it, only still more agonizing suffering and death. This deception tortured him—their not wishing to admit what they all knew and what he knew, but wanting to lie to him concerning his terrible condition, and wishing and forcing him to participate in that lie. Those lies—lies enacted over him on the eve of his death and destined to degrade this awful, solemn act to the level of their visitings, their curtains, their sturgeon for dinner—*

were a terrible agony for Ivan Ilych. And strangely enough, many times when they were going through their antics over him he had been within a hairbreadth of calling out to them: "Stop lying! You know and I know that I am dying. Then at least stop lying about it!" But he had never had the spirit to do it. The awful, terrible act of his dying was, he could see, reduced by those about him to the level of a casual, unpleasant, and almost indecorous incident (as if someone entered a drawing-room diffusing an unpleasant odour).

Case 15

Fred R., aged twenty-three, applied for a medical homemaker to take care of his mother. Mrs. R. was sixty years old, had cancer of the lung with metastasis to the brain. She was constantly dizzy and, since she had lost the use of her arm, she couldn't bathe or dress herself without help. Although she couldn't go up and down stairs from her bedroom, her independent nature rebelled against any assistance, which meant that someone in the family would have to be in constant attendance should she want to go to the bathroom or use the stairs.

To make matters worse, her retired husband of sixty-four was ordered by his doctor to use the stairs only once a day. This limitation, along with cataracts, made it virtually impossible for him to give much help to his wife.

So the son, Fred, had to assume most of the burden of care for his mother and run the household, thus being unable to look for a job. This made Mrs. R. very unhappy for him, especially as a married older son was finding it very difficult to help her financially while he had to support his own family and business.

After Mrs. R. finally decided to accept outside help, the agency helped to pay for a medical homemaker, and Fred was now free to accept a job three weeks later. The homemaker not only made it possible for Fred's eighteen-year-old premed brother to continue his studies, but allowed Mr. R. to resume his former pattern of lunching with friends and playing cards.

Since the medical homemaker devoted her whole time to caring for Mrs. R., the sons could find time to market and do household chores.

Case 20

In September of last year, fifteen-year-old Mark S. had a diagnosis of Hodgkin's Disease of the fourth stage. Although experimental drugs were being used, his prognosis was poor.

Neither Mark's father nor his younger sister knew the diagnosis. Because his mother had been described as mentally unstable and institutionalized several times, Mark's father had custody of the children and resented the fact that his wife's unannounced visits upset them considerably.

Although Mr. S. was extremely worried about his son's illness, he came to the agency office only once and could not bring himself to talk about Mark's condition and his own feelings. He also used every means to keep the truth from his son because he was afraid it would make Mark "give up."

Owing to the drugs and the placement of a five-day, seven-hour homemaker, Mark began to improve after a few months, but subsequently had to be rehospitalized. At this point his father finally turned to the agency for advice and support, using the telephone for regular interviews in which he could finally acknowledge his feelings of grief and guilt, and admitted that Mark probably knew he was dying. During the period when Mark was alternately in and out of the hospital, Mr. S. finally brought himself to talk openly to his son about his illness and its inevitable course. Mark chose to return home, where he died a few weeks later.

After his death, Mr. S. expressed his gratitude for the homemaker and for being helped by the agency to face the truth and share it with Mark. He said he felt this honesty had made his son's death more dignified, and that their relationship before it had become much closer. Mr. S. had even been able to expunge his bitterness toward Mark's mother and could even feel pity for her now.

Case 31

A year ago, Mr. K. called the agency for advice. A diagnosis had been made six months before that his wife had cancer of the colon with liver metastasis, and that in spite of chemotherapy her prognosis, which she was told but did not fully take in, was from six months to a year.

According to Mr. K., a dentist, his wife functions normally when she is without pain and looks well in spite of a slight weight loss. A former speech therapist, she has tried not to change their family routine in spite of what lay ahead for them both.

Mr. K.'s main worry is that the conflict between the needs of their three children and his deep involvement with his wife's condition is building up tensions in the home that never existed before, even though both of them spend as much time as possible with their son and two daughters.

According to the agency, both husband and wife seem to have a very close and warm relationship, sharing equally in every respect of their lives and household. But what worries him deeply now is the frequent depressions that assail his wife more and more as time goes on. Mrs. K. cries frequently and says why "is this happening to me," and all her husband can do, he says, is to tell her not to give up hope, to say how well she's doing, and—sometimes—just hold her and cry with her.

The younger children know that their mother is sick but not that she may die. But since her grandfather's recent death, the older daughter has talked about dying and once said, "it will either be Dad or Mommy next." Mr. K. said that all he could do was simply to say that "all of us die someday, Betty."

Case 48

Last fall Miss E. called the agency for a homemaker because she had had a double mastectomy and the cancer had spread to her spine and pelvis. At forty-two she was virtually bedridden, living only on disability pay.

At the first signs of cancer, Miss E. had gone into therapy, which she said had helped a lot in dealing with her conflicting feelings about herself, and also with the man who left her when he heard she had cancer. She even began to learn to walk again with crutches, determined to take care of her mother, who had hardening of the arteries, and by so doing "come out of herself."

Her main frustration, however, was having to stay home after years of an absorbing job as a television news editor. Because of this, she accepted the offer of a business friend to take a part-time job in his office. Not only were her hours very flexible, but a homemaker made it possible to work for a few hours every day and then find help and care on returning home. She has told the agency that without this homemaker, even this relatively brief "escape" and change would be impossible. Miss E.'s philosophy, she said, has always been, "trying is living."

These are four typical examples from three different agencies dedicated to health care in cases of catastrophic illnesses. By emphasizing the treatment of *the whole family*, they incorporate a new concept that should be of significant help in the terminal phase and after.

This treatment, or therapy, has now become a major concern of psychiatrists, churchmen, social workers, and organizations like the Foundation of Thanatology (dedicated to the study of death and dying in all its aspects). Largely due to their increasing involvement, special sessions are being conducted in hospitals for free exchange between the staff and the relatives of chronically or seriously ill patients.

For indeed, death is as much a trauma for the living and the loving as it is for the dying. It is even more of a trauma if they reject it or the possibility of it.

As her companion of thirty or forty years, it is agonizing for a husband to watch the steady erosion of his wife from cancer: the waxy skin, the merging skeleton of what was once a vital and full-bodied woman. Love struggles with revulsion and shames him into touching her hand or forehead in signals of comfort. Compassion forces him to tell her she's "looking better," when it is a palpable lie.

Very few are like a pharmacist friend of mine whose wife, his constant companion in home as well as work, contracted cancer in her fifties.

She knew it, he knew it. It was a kind of cancer that weakened rather than stabbed: she continued to stand behind the counter most days of the week, her warmth and smile investing every small service to those who bought. In contrast, her husband played tough-guy, fooling none.

Then she started being in the store only three days a week . . . then two . . . then none.

Worried, I asked Lew what was the matter and he told me. They lived in a small apartment right over the store, so he kept in constant touch with her. A diabetic himself, in frequent pain, he led two exhausting lives. And one week when he himself no longer appeared in the store, I knew that only Letty's death was the reason.

I asked him afterward how it was. "We've loved each other for over thirty years," said Lew. "We've borne two fine sons. We've had a great life. It has to end, doesn't it?

"We knew it would. Letty knew. Near the end, when she began to feel real bad, we rushed her to the hospital. They gave her some new chemotherapy. It made her very sick.

"Back home, I could help her in some ways, of course. But she never really thought about death.

"She died one night, at home, without pain.

"But I want to tell you something," Lew added. "She hasn't been left alone this whole month for a single second. Her brother, our sons, her nieces and nephews, my brother—one of them's always been near her night and day—even when I can't be with her. She was the most loved woman I ever knew."

The two salient points in the case of Lew and Letty are 1) that they both knew the score right from the beginning and talked of it freely, and 2) that she died at home in the constant presence of those who loved her.

The increasing percentage of people who die in hospitals (two-thirds, by current estimates) are not surrounded by those they love. The moment of death finds grieving relatives—none of them children—in waiting rooms. Even if those under seventeen *were* allowed in hospitals, most families would hesitate to "subject" them to this painful experience. The body is then whisked away for mortuary services and seen again only by such relatives who prefer funerals where the cosmeticized face of their loved one is visible on satin quilting in an expensive coffin.

But what has happened before the seriously ill reach the hospital or when they are cared for in their homes till they die?

Many different things, in a nation of such diversity and so little cohesion that most generalizations founder. Only worry, grief, alarm, and deprivation are universal.

Bereavement, of course: an enveloping trauma of loss that is seldom counterbalanced—at least at first—by a sense of relief at the end of suffering in the one who died. In some, a continuing disbelief that this being, so close, so intimately known for so long, really is no more, has gone, will not return.

In some, guilt too. For not doing more, for not being more, for not loving more.

In some, a concealed relief at the lifting of personal and financial burdens too great to bear. In plain terms, a registered nurse costs $150 a day for twenty-four-hour home care, the fee for daily intensive-care nurses is $231, and the most reasonable solution, a live-in home health aide, comes to $189 a week.

Far more anguishing to those families invested with love is the question of truth: whether to tell the one in their midst—or even at the hospital—what they themselves know, informed by the doctor, or what they suspect.

A family as close as Lew and Letty's could not, would not, deceive each other. The honesty that had held them together so long could not now be withheld, either from wife or children.

But for most of us it is a ticklish question, answered only by another question. Does the victim of fatal illness really *want* to know? How deep are the defenses against that kind of truth? This bedevils doctors and psychiatrists as much as it does the family. After a fatal medical prognosis, what do you tell them? Do you try to soothe them with hope—or merely keep silent?

Of those in contact with the fatally ill, their family should know them best: should know when the dying know, and respond accordingly.

"Please—I want to know my chances. . . . Please!" To evade an urgent question with a bland evasion is almost as cruel as the isolation of silence, diminishing not only the trust but the dignity of dying.

"I don't want to die! Please tell me I won't die." What do you say? "We're doing everything we can to see that you don't"? "None of us can tell you that . . ."? "Don't think about it, think about getting well"? Tortured, you play it by ear.

Or you cannot face it at all. You don't even tell the children. Keep them away from death: keep them away from life. Close the door to the sickroom.

Especially at the end. The sight of the dead might be too great a shock. Perhaps. In the old especially there can be the hint of skeleton in bones which the skin barely covers. There is also—often—an astounding serenity in the faces of many: the patina of final peace. If the young cannot see this, they cannot learn abiding truth.

Perhaps analogies and images might help them, prepare them for the shock of fear of this sight. Bare trees in winter: the long sleep, a kind of death. Rock pinnacles in mountain country: strong wonderful shapes, forced by nature's convulsions and deaths. You show a child a shell—now empty of life, but no less beautiful.

You say: "Look at this face of the aunt you loved. She escaped her body."

For the patient where consciousness still lingers, the intimacy of home can be far more sustaining than a hospital bed. Desirable as this familiar cocoon may be, however, the current logistics of living work against it.

The rich with rooms to spare in house or apartment are a minority in our society. Yet even they seek smaller and more convenient quarters when their children are gone and their husbands retire. And the trend toward the smaller "nuclear" family has contracted the space even middle-class families can spare for the privacy of a chronically ill parent or relative.

More often than not it is the poor minority groups, black or ethnic, who still contain life in all its stages in their cramped dwellings. Whether a wooden shack in the South or a tenement apartment in the North, the place is bursting with generations of kin. Birth and death coexist equally, accepted, welcomed, or mourned. Death has no special status, is no surprise. It is simply a fact of life.

Somehow room is made for the dying, as room is made for the sixth—and often unwished for—baby. Three on a bed, two on a cot—for the very poor this is not by desire but by circumstance over which the helpless and ignorant have no control. Those who need not live this way are appalled. Those who do have a kind of cohesion that the more fortunate seem to be losing.

Primitive societies, pockets of them still living in remote jungles or plains, make short shrift of death, take it in their stride with ritual or chant. The tribe is the family: all take part in the passage and passing of life.

It may be that the privacy so dear to the civilized and economically secure has, in banishing communal ritual and common experience, made acceptance of death intolerable.

V

The New Therapy

When Sigmund Freud at seventy-two accepted young Doctor Schur as his personal internist, he stipulated that Schur would never lie to him, and then said, "Promise me. When the time comes, you won't let me suffer unnecessarily." (About his own dying father, Freud had said years before: "The unconscious is immortal.")

In 1939, after eleven years of acute suffering and countless operations on his cancerous mouth (added to the horror of Hitler's rise and Freud's own unremitting work), the time came. Now in English exile, the great psychoanalyst was not only too pain-racked to read, let alone write, but necrosis of the tissue emanated an odor so foul that his own long-loved dog lay twenty feet away, and even those dearest to him could barely endure to come close.

Freud then gave the word to Schur, and Schur gave him two injections of morphine, one at night and one in the early morning. By contemporary standards they were light doses. But since Freud had refused all pain killers through his many cancerous bouts, the drug brought death.

Schur, as his own brilliant psychobiography of Freud made clear, was constant witness to the struggle in this creative genius between the life force and the death wish.

The same struggle now is widely manifest in those psychiatrists who have to deal with it not only in themselves, but in professional contact with the dying.

They are as yet a relatively small band. The reasons are clear. Their profession is oriented to the healing or strengthening of the psyche so that it can withstand not only the pressures of external life but the anxieties of the inner self. It is aimed toward the patient's fullest realization of self, of his powers as well as his limitations, and toward an acceptance of truth that will free the hitherto shackled or impeded spirit. It is therefore deeply concerned with ongoing life.

Yet with the great lengthening of the human life span, and the growing numbers of the fatally ill suspended in limbo to await their end with little spiritual comfort or support, some psychiatrists now feel impelled to come to their aid, to ease the final transition.

They seem to agree on only three points. One is the need to strengthen the vital force by supporting their patient's sense of identity as an individual. The second (essential to the first) is to listen to them. And the third consensus is that the psychiatrists themselves cannot psychically sustain in their practice more than a few patients near death. "It is a terrible strain," said one of them, "because in order to communicate with the dying, we must ourselves understand—and try to feel—the process of dying."

It is because of this, and because the attitudes of the family toward this process can deeply affect the doomed patient, that psychiatrists find the counseling of relatives so important.

They know what it can do to a husband aware of his cancer to have a wife who never mentions it. The physical pain can be tempered by drugs, but for the pain of isolation there is no anodyne.

They know that if close family members cannot bring themselves to share the truth gently with those they are about to lose, then they must share it with a neutral but compassionate ear.

This ear need not be the psychiatrist's alone. In fact, very few of us can afford his counsel, either in time or money. The psychiatrists themselves lack the firm base of knowledge in the psychic aspects of death that the doctor possesses in biological terms. One of their most eloquent spokesmen, Dr. Avery D. Weisman, concedes that psychosocial data on dying are not only very elusive, but much more difficult to obtain than observations about organic disease. An aged person may live for years in a chronic hospital, but his interests, actions, and ordinary habits are neither observed nor recorded.

Weisman also observes, as I have myself found in chronic and terminal wards, that the higher the professional rank of staff members, the less familiar they are with patients as people.

A fascinating sidelight was a study made recently (and surreptitiously) by a young psychologist in the geriatric ward of a big city hospital. Having counseled a patient there, he had acquainted himself with the numbers of the rooms that housed those on the critical list. He spent several hours one night in view of the call-board signaling requests from patients by means of lights for nursing attention. After comparing these calls with the room numbers on his chart and the time it took for them to be answered, he saw—unequivocally—

that the nearer the patient was to death, the longer the wait for nursing response.

The floor knew the score. Old Mrs. Jones always called just for company, or some trivial thing. Old Mr. Smith didn't know what he was doing anymore. Miss Schwartz was a chronic complainer.

This tardy response from the nurses wasn't deliberate callousness: more a feeling of uselessness at this stage of the game. Those with a chance for life deserved priority.

Like many of us, inside and outside of the health professions, psychiatrist Kurt Eissler has noticed that all modern medicine has achieved is to make it more difficult for man to die, "although his preoccupation with his body, his worry about disease have not decreased. It may even have been augmented."

It is this worry, this call for help in the night or the day, that the "lower echelons" in the treatment hierarchy of the critically ill are now trying to answer.

Again in the death of Ivan Ilych, it was his humble servant Gerasim—holding his aching body, sharing his agony—who gave any comfort or peace. And those who have seen Ingmar Bergman's *Cries and Whispers* know that in this elaborate family mansion, cold and dark with unspoken words and ungiven love, it was the maid who held her cancer-ridden mistress to her breast, rocking and soothing her until the convulsive end.

So now, social workers, young aides, and unorthodox ministers sit at the bedside of the near-to-death to listen, to comfort, to pray—if asked to—to touch, to answer. They are also open to bewildered or agonized relatives in need of counsel and direction.

The growing trend is for less specialization, more interdependence in this ultimate care. Doctors, interns, and nurses should share their knowledge and observations with their subordinates instead of proceeding in virtual ignorance of each other's decisions and actions.

So far, only one out of a hundred private hospitals intimately involved with catastrophic disease and terminal care have established training courses for this new form of "consciousness raising." For one thing, they go against the grain of the medical hierarchy. For another, they are rejected by the hospital unions, who do not want to join any training program with management.

Since union members die as well as doctors, the familiar and fruitless act of cutting off the nose to spite the face is with us again. Or is it perhaps the territorial imperative? The turf?

Whatever the resistance, courses for this new kind of group counseling are being held under the auspices of the Foundation of Thanatology, Cancer Care, and other institutions dedicated to the study and alleviation of critical or terminal diseases ravishing human beings.

Last year the Foundation of Thanatology, spearheaded by its founder Dr. Austin Kutscher, held a conference at Columbia University devoted largely to this counseling. One session included psychiatrists, priests, nurses, doctors, and social workers.

They appeared to agree on several salient points, among them that city hospitals were largely dumping grounds for training doctors and for dying patients on Medicare and Medicaid, and of necessity often brutalized by their own bureaucracy. To reverse this trend, it was suggested that doctors should regain their philosophic control of hospitals, making them more human and less mechanical.

The conferees could not know that scarcely two months after this discussion the American Hospital Association, based in Chicago, would establish a patient's "Bill of Rights" which would include, among the twelve major points, the right to "obtain from his physician complete, current information concerning his diagnosis, treatment, and prognosis in terms the patient can reasonably hope to understand . . . the right to refuse treatment to the extent permitted by law, and to be informed of the medical consequences of his action . . . and the right to receive from his physician information necessary to give informed consent prior to the start of any procedure and/or treatment."

All these rights, moreover, to include the guarantee of total privacy between patient, doctor, and hospital staff. Most importantly, copies of these rights to be given to every patient entering or in the hospital.

Following this patient's Bill of Rights in a matter of days was a statement from the New York State Medical Society which, though prohibiting doctors from authorizing mercy killings, supported a patient's "right" to die with dignity if he so chooses; adding that when "there is irrefutable evidence that biological death is inevitable," this right must be "the joint decision of the patient and/or the immediate family with the approval of the family physician."

The door was open at last. But only ajar.

VI
What Is Death?

Departed to the judgment,
A mighty afternoon;
Great clouds like ushers leaning,
Creation looking on.

The flesh surrendered, cancelled,
The bodiless begun;
Two worlds, like audiences, disperse
And leave the soul alone.

Emily Dickinson

Death is the end of life. If I live I am. If I die I am not. Death is nonbeing.

Death is the end of consciousness. Death is when the brain stops functioning, when the heart stops beating, when the breath expires.

What is this? Seldom a spoken dialogue in our society. The British historian Arnold Toynbee wrote that "Death is un-American, an affront to every citizen's inalienable right to life, liberty, and the pursuit of happiness." He was not entirely joking. As noted before, we do not like to talk about it even when it is seldom absent from the minds of the sick or the old or from those who love them or tend them.

Yet since the beginning of recorded history, others have repeatedly tried to come to terms with the meaning of death. Socrates said that "death may be the greatest of all human blessings"; Seneca that "death is sometimes a punishment, often a gift, and to many, a favor."

Death was a constant presence in Shakespeare's plays, and sociologist Georg Simmel observed over fifty years ago that "In Shakespeare's great tragic figures we sense almost from their first words the inevitability of their end. This is not seen, however, as an inability to untangle the threads of destiny, or as a threatening fate, but as a deep necessity . . . a property of their total inner life which is woven into the dramatic, finally lethal event. . . .

"In contrast, subordinate figures die in these tragedies as the external course of events brings it about. . . . Only those others are allowed to die from within: the maturation of their destinies as an expression of life is per se the maturation of their deaths."

> . . . And nothing can we call our own but
>   death;
> And that small model of the barren earth,
> Which serves as paste and cover to our bones.

Thus Shakespeare in *King Richard II*, and this in *King Lear*:

> Vex not his ghost: O! let him pass! he hates him
> That would upon the rack of this tough world
> Stretch him out longer.

And in our time? Many brave and eloquent men have looked death squarely in the face. "My bags are packed," said Pope John XXIII in 1965. "I am ready to go."

But now the open dialogue of death is far more pragmatic than poetic because machines control the timing —*and* definition—of death.

It has become medically, legally, and morally imperative to determine the moment of death now that the growing movement for euthanasia and the increasing use of organ transplants demand precise and irrefutable criteria.

An examination of the many concurrent attempts, both here and abroad, to establish these criteria, show that they all agree on one point: the definition of persistent heart failure is no longer an adequate definition of death. The death of the brain, more specifically called "irreversible coma," is now widely accepted as the cessation of life.

Dr. Henry K. Beecher, chairman of a committee at Harvard composed of members of five faculties in the university, explains the rudiments of this definition: "The individual who has irreversible coma is deeply unconscious, with no response to external stimuli or to internal need. There are no movements, there is no breathing, there is no reflex activity except in some cases through the spinal cord. Almost everybody else has required the use of the electroencephalogram. We think it helps confirmatory evidence, but do not think it is necessary by itself. Specifically excluded are individuals who are under central nervous system depressants, or whose internal temperature is below 96 degrees Fahrenheit.

"Now these requirements that I mentioned must persist over at least a 24-hour period."

Dr. Beecher supports these findings with evidence from his own respiratory unit at Massachusetts General Hospital, and a separate study of 1,662 individuals who had isoelectric encephalograms (EEG's) over twenty-four hours or more, not one of whom recovered.

He observes too that we are entering a new era in medicine "where to do nothing is far more radical than to do something," and quotes a report of the death in Montreal of a twenty-one-year-old woman who had been unconscious since a traffic accident twelve years earlier, a procedure which he estimates kept 312 patients out of a hospital bed.

We have here the results of the tragic paradox: keeping this woman's body alive with machines was "doing something," where turning off the machines would have been the "radical" act of doing nothing (except freeing the spirit as well as the hospital bed?).

Anyone who has seen the encephalogram of a dying patient must recognize a startling symbolism. The small white objects darting on waves along the black screen and finally leveling out in a straight line after lower and lower peaks of brain activity—these are identical in shape and motion to the wriggling sperm of life.

Their flattening out is biological death. Yet to each level of life there is a counterpart of nonexistence that is another kind of death, no less measurable in human terms. Dr. Biorck, a Swedish physician, defines these as 1) social death, when mobility, freedom of action and choice are supplanted by dependence, isolation, and loneliness; 2) spiritual death, when intellectual activity and emotional vigor founder in a lost memory and a vacant mind; 3) vegetative and metabolic death: organs and cells kept alive by machines, disintegration, finally, after the "person" has, in fact, died.

Inevitably, one returns to that indefinable entity

called the "soul." In a report issued by the Foundation of Thanatology some doctors claimed to have found evidence of an element of the mystical in the experience of patients still conscious. The doctors are quick to say that they are not talking about God and religion and parapsychological cultism; also they admit that such experiences might be the result of anoxia, or oxygen starvation of the brain. Nevertheless, they say, there is reason to believe that the dying can experience a sense of surrender that borders on ecstasy. . . . In the safety of anonymity, they return again and again to the puzzle of what it is that dies when the body ceases to function.

One doctor, attempting to describe the mystery he had sensed in dying patients, quoted the last words attributed to the ancient philosopher Plotinus: "I am making my last effort to return that which is divine in me to that which is divine in the universe."

It is ironic that this effort is still being thwarted by the two great—and usually conflicting—forces: the mighty new powers of science and the ancient domination of the Church. The first, by its very nature, has not and cannot concern itself with morality. The mind capable of creating atomic fission is not the mind ordering its use to kill millions of humans. The enlargement of human knowledge of this vast universe is inevitable, whether it becomes blessing or curse.

Yet the great religious institutions of our civilization have been, and still are, committed to moral definition and imposition: what is Good and what is Evil. And although they too are changing through the pressures of social upheaval from without and gradual erosion from within, their concepts of life and death and human behavior still form the patterns of collective conscience and custom in most non-Communist states of the world.

VII
The Good Death

My dread, my ignorance, my
Self, it is time. Your imminence
Prowls the palms of my hands like sweat.
Do not now, if I rise to welcome you,
Make off like roads into the deep night.
The dogs are dead at last, the locks toothless,
The habits out of reach.
I will not be false to you tonight.

Come, no longer unthinkable. Let us share
Understanding like a family name. Bring
Integrity as a gift, something
Which I had lost, which you found on the way.
I will lay it beside us, the old knife,
While we reach our conclusions.

Come. As a man who hears a sound at the gate
Opens the window and puts out the light
The better to see out into the dark,
Look, I put it out.

"Finally," by W. S. Merwin

Euthanasia is a word that conjures up—still, in many people—almost as much fear as death itself. It is one thing to translate the Greek word into "the good death"; it is another to clear away the confusions about what, exactly, this apparently benign term means.

Is it something you do to yourself: suicide? Is it something others do to you: murder? Could it even be a polite synonym for genocide: mass killing of the innocent, young or old, who happen to be burdens on society?

Euthanasia is none of these things. It is simply to be able to die with dignity at a moment when life is devoid of it. It is a purely voluntary choice, both on the part of the owner of this life and on the part of the doctor who knows that this is no longer a life.

Euthanasia is the chosen alternative to the prolongation of a steadily waning mind and spirit by machines that withhold death or to an existence that mocks life.

For the doctor, it is the passive or negative act of refraining from measures that in his opinion would sustain merely a marginal or vegetable existence. That he would be influenced by the express wish of a conscious patient to "let go" seems reasonable, though the decision is, and must be, primarily his own.

Suicide, whether approved by others or not, is the most solitary human choice. The definition of it as rational or irrational is entirely arbitrary.

As for mercy killings, they are dual acts. One human being helps another to end intolerable suffering; sometimes on the single initiative of compassion and horror, more often in response to the pleas of the sufferer. Mercy is not strained.

And abortion? Here the choice is complex, involving mother, doctor, and unborn fetus. In the case of a fetus found to be so severely damaged in brain or body or both that its birth would mean merely a vegetable life, the termination of this life could indeed be called "the good death." The only difference between the vegetable old and the vegetable young is the length of time inexorably facing the child and its stricken parents.

We are in many ways a violent society, reacting violently to various forms of oppression, real or presumed, by official fiat or human prejudice. But a nation in which capital punishment even for major crimes is increasingly rare would find it hard to justify the killing of its political or social rejects in the name of euthanasia.

We would do better as citizens to exchange such apocalyptic fears of possible ultimate evil for the increasing realities of a possible ultimate good.

The idea of euthanasia has been a long time coming.

In all societies, the structure of power of state or Church has consistently rejected any idea likely to give the individual power of choice in matters of life and death, or freedom of action in accord with his own private conscience. The only way any ruling establishment until recent times has been able to maintain its sovereignty, in fact, has been able to keep people within frameworks of legal and religious patterns which may once have served society well, but have now—in the light of mighty convulsions—ceased to be either applicable or useful in human terms.

Yet single courageous voices have never been stilled. In 1624, John Donne, the Dean of St. Paul's, wrote an essay in support of euthanasia asking "whether it was logical to conscript a young man and subject him to risk of torture and mutilation in war and probable death, and refuse an old man escape from an agonizing end."

Even earlier Sir Thomas More, eminent Catholic, wrote in the second book of his *Utopia* that in his imaginary community "when any is taken with a torturing and lingering pain, so that there is no hope either of cure or ease, the priests and magistrates come and exhort them, that, since they are not able to go on with the business of life, are becoming a burden to themselves and all about them, and they have really outlived themselves, they should no longer nourish such a rooted distemper, but choose rather to die since they cannot live but in much misery."

And in his *New Atlantis,* Francis Bacon wrote: "I esteem it the office of a physician not only to restore health, but to mitigate pain and dolours; and not only when such mitigation may conduce to recovery, but when it may serve to make a fair and easy passage."

"A fair and easy passage." Less than a century ago, anesthetics to ease the passage of birth or the pain of an operation were considered offenses against "God's will" by the pious.

In 1847, an Edinburgh physician gave ether to women in labor, a year after Massachusetts General Hospital in Boston began using it in surgery. He was attacked by the profession, laity, and clergy, who claimed that the pains of labor were appointed to the lot of women by divine decree, and that it was sacrilegious to use means for their relief.

"It is a decoy of Satan," intoned a minister of the Gospel, "apparently offering itself to bless woman, but in the end will harden society and rob God of the deep, earnest cries for help which arise in time of trouble." The good minister, of course, had never given birth.

Neither have legislators opposing abortion, nor, since they are clearly not at death's door, those opposing euthanasia.

Church and state are simply continuing the kind of attacks made in turn by their supporters against vaccination, the ligation of arteries, the telescope, and the microscope. Anything, in fact, that might alter the prevailing attitudes toward the meaning of life or death, or extend human perception.

And yet long before Christ, Greek mythology encouraged Greeks suffering from incurable ailments to entreat Thanatos, the god of death, to free them from their misery.

And long after Christ, in our first years as a nation, Benjamin Franklin, referring to man's painful end, said, "We have very great pity for an animal if we see it in agonies and death throes. We put it out of its misery no matter how noble the animal."

Basically, the core of this unending argument is the contradiction implicit in the Hippocratic Oath, which promises two things: first, to relieve suffering, and second, to prolong and protect life. Yet often the prolongation of life can increase pain; and the relief of pain can shorten life.

Since the Hippocratic Oath was defined in 400 B.C. and in increasing numbers of medical colleges is no longer required, many doctors might turn gratefully to the law to help them resolve this acute dilemma of conscience. But attempts to enact legislation permitting voluntary euthanasia within strict and clearly defined limits and conditions have been struck down in Great Britain successively in parliamentary debates of 1936, 1950, and 1969, and in the New York State Legislature in 1947. This particular bill was underwritten by almost two thousand physicians and fifty-four clergy, the latter denounced by the 1947 American Council of Christian Churches as "evidence that the modernistic clergy have made further departure from the eternal moral law."

Since the unsuccessful New York State bill of 1947 was a simpler version of the first British attempt to introduce legal euthanasia, it might be illuminating to give the essence of the last debate in the House of Lords in 1969 on the "good death."

(It is wryly typical of British mores that Lord Raglan's powerful arguments for euthanasia were preceded by an amendment offered by a Lord Hughes that "will have the effect of repealing completely the present order authorising the use of gin traps against both foxes and otters. The order will not be repealed only in so far as it applies to otters, which I am sure was the intention of the noble Lord, Lord Burton.")

After mentioning the previous efforts to legalize euthanasia, Lord Raglan said:

"I think that I have good reason to believe that opinion generally has become so favourable to a change in the law that the time is ripe, not to bring a Motion to test your Lordships' opinion but to introduce another Bill incorporating changes in the proposed formalities and safeguards, which I think were rightly criticised in the previous Bill, and which I, with some confidence, hope your Lordships will think a sound basis for legislation. When my noble friend Lord Longford was criticising the Abortion Bill he made a prophecy that it would be 'euthanasia next.' In fact, it was quite a safe prophecy to make, because this Bill, as I see it, is one in line with recent measures, such as the Suicide Act and others, which betoken a change of attitude in our society towards the freedom of the individual."

Raglan went on to observe that there was now less inclination for the state to legislate in areas of private conscience and behavior than before, and that in fact there was growing demand for repeal or modification of existing laws that seemed unduly restrictive of private choice.

He found it surprising that voluntary euthanasia had not already become legal, and believed the main reason for this was that those who most wished for it—the old and infirm—could not of necessity wage an energetic and articulate campaign.

"Those who suffer and die slowly," said Raglan, "may not have much to say for themselves; and death itself is the most private experience of all."

This introductory statement was followed by eight major clauses:

Clause 1 provides that a physician may administer euthanasia to a "qualified patient" who has made a declaration in the form set out in the schedule. A qualified patient is defined as a patient over the age of majority who has been certified by two physicians, one being of consultant status, to be apparently suffering from an irremediable condition.

Clause 2 provides that a declaration shall come into force thirty days after being made, and shall remain in force for three years. A declaration reexecuted within the twelve months preceding its expiry date shall remain in force for life, unless revoked.

Clause 3 provides that a declaration may be revoked at any time.

Clause 4 provides that before euthanasia may be given to a mentally responsible patient the physician in charge must ascertain to the best of his ability that the declaration and steps proposed to be taken under it accord with the patient's wishes. Subsection (2) provides that a nurse, acting on the directions of a physician, may cause euthanasia to be administered to a patient, and subsection (3) provides that no physician or nurse who is opposed on principle to euthanasia shall be required to take any steps in its administration.

Clause 5 protects physicians and nurses who act in good faith in the belief that their actions are in accordance with a patient's declaration or further requests made under the Act and provides that they *shall not be in breach of any professional oath by administering euthanasia.*

Clause 6 provides that a person who conceals, destroys, falsifies, or forges a declaration commits an offense punishable by life imprisonment and that an attesting witness who willfully makes a false statement commits an offense punishable by up to seven years' imprisonment.

Clause 7 provides that euthanasia shall not, except in limited circumstances, invalidate any insurance policy.

Clause 8 declares that all terminal patients are entitled to receive whatever quantity of drugs may be required to keep them entirely free from pain; and that in a case where severe distress cannot be alleviated by pain-killing drugs, the patient is entitled, if he so desires, to be made and kept entirely unconscious. The section applies to patients whether or not they have made any declaration, and is expressed to be for the removal of doubt as to the existing state of the law.

The clauses were followed in turn by a detailed definition of all terms involved, including "physician," "qualified patient," "irremediable condition," and so forth.

Although Raglan's bill was supported by a substantial minority, some criticized it as being too cumbersome or restrictive both for lawyers and doctors, believing that a simplified version would attain its ends without such complex means.

Others continued to view any efforts to legalize euthanasia, however guarded, as the "thin edge of the wedge."

Simply, it means that any departure from, or intrusion of, the statutes of common law that we inherited from the British and incorporated into our own Constitution, is a violation of basic ethics and an invitation to evil. In the context of euthanasia, "mercy killing" of the dying becomes simply murder, and suicide, self-murder.

The religious objection is, of course, founded on the Sixth Commandment, commonly translated as "Thou shalt not kill," but actually phrased in the Book of Common Prayer as "Thou shalt do no murder."

In both cases it is assumed that any act terminating a life from motives of mercy or compassion can—if permitted by law—be inspired as well by evil motives.

We come here to a curious anomaly. Mass killing as in war is not included in these pulpit strictures against "murder." Since supreme domination over life belongs to God alone, God alone may authorize man to kill, although in the words of the Reverend Joseph V. Sullivan, "today there is no indication that God is giving anyone orders to kill the innocent."

"Innocent" apparently does not apply to a combatant opposing a nation "that is fighting a just war, or an unjust aggressor."

This might explain the ardor with which two eminent American churchmen, the late Cardinal Spellman, and his successor Cardinal Cooke, supported our war in Vietnam while saying prayers for thousands of American dead. No prayers were said for the several million "unjust aggressors" killed by Americans.

This continuing paradox of the "wedge" principle (the assumption that every new concept, however benevolent in purpose, can also serve malign ends) would make it impossible to draw the line, because the line would have to be pushed further and further back until all action, for benign as well as evil motives, would be outlawed.

John Donne would have had no part of this: ". . . to chuse is to do: but to be no part of any body, that is to be nothing."

To be part of somebody is to feel for somebody. Some call this compassion, some empathy. If either is felt, benevolent action must proceed from it. It is hard to imagine that evil ends impel a doctor to remove the life supports of a dying patient. What malicious intent would prompt a physician to administer sedatives to ease terminal pain, knowing that nevertheless they might shorten the patient's life? The physician gains nothing from the death of a patient except a sense, perhaps, of defeat or—if the patient is a friend—of loss.

Cynics might suspect that some relatives might encourage the hastening of death not only because of the emotional and financial burdens of sustaining a flickering, helpless life, but for a hastened inheritance.

Yet even in such venial cases, feelings of guilt would probably deter action and be expiated by the greater burden of watching prolonged human deterioration. The doctor now hears, "Please don't do anything more" far oftener than he did ten years ago. And thousands of doctors now answer the plea.

My brother and I asked this of our family physician as the ninety-two-year-old father we loved so much was losing all substance except for his wish to die.

"Why must I go on?" he asked me one day. "Why?" And when I saw the stern Lutheran nurse who had replaced his former gentle companion try to force food into his mouth while he tried in vain to turn his face away, no doubts lingered. The doctor ordered the end of all artificial sustenance and chemical injections and our father was answered with death.

This was, of course, one form of passive euthanasia: doing nothing to help sustain a guttering life. A life, in this case, bereft of joy, of will, of consciousness most of the time, and of the music which, along with a wife now ten years dead, were his imperative supports.

There are many variations of this "letting go." One doctor, knowing that one of his patients had no hope of survival, sent him home from the hospital on the grounds that he would be happier in familiar surroundings. Withdrawn from all artificial life supports, he died a week later, "quietly," said his wife, "in his sleep."

An elderly internist who treated an old friend of mine told me about G.'s last months. "As you know," he said, "G. had long been a diabetic, injecting himself daily with insulin before I treated him for leukemia. He was going on with his work, as well as he could, and coming to me every week for these new injections. In spite of them, of course, he grew progressively weaker until one day he turned up at my office, gray-faced, and said, 'Let me go. I am so tired. I don't want any more injections.'

"Because I not only loved but respected him greatly, I said, 'All right.' He died two weeks later, at home, in peace."

In both of these cases, the quality of life and not its extension was the overriding determinant. To certain individuals—usually those who have led full, demanding, and stimulating lives—the slow, inexorable reduction of their capacities is worse than death.

Possibly these are still a minority. Anyone in close contact with the long-term and critically ill will tell you that the will to live—consciously or unconsciously, and on whatever crippling or diminishing terms—is tenacious. The wards and nursing homes of this nation are full of half-lives, sustained by this tenacity.

The inference here might be that those who opt for life on any terms have never known life in its fullest terms. One of many alarming facts of our current society is the steady erosion of quality in the face of quantity. Too many people, surrounded by too many things, have too little. Not in terms of worldly goods but in the conscious savoring of the hours and days of their lives. Millions have never lived to their fullest capacities. And because of this, they would settle rather for a minimal life than no life at all. Their dread of death supersedes all else.

In sharp contrast are those human beings endowed since youth with a strong sense of purpose, of mission. For every genius in history who died young after fulfilling a creative destiny, there are a great number of individuals of marked attainments in the arts and sciences and government who, at whatever age, die soon after they can no longer function in their chosen work. They may have loving mates and children, but their impotence as productive beings is the paramount factor. In effect, they say, "My work is done." Their death is close to an act of will.

In the last twenty years we have seen this will thwarted by medical science, in the name of respect and even compassion, by keeping two Presidents half-alive far beyond their human needs or competence. The long-drawn-out ends of Eisenhower and Truman divested them both of the dignity of timely death. And although they were very different men, one could reasonably suspect that neither of them would have consciously chosen to die in the trap of machines and meaningless time.

Among humbler mortals, the element of will or choice takes another form. Especially in devoted and long-married couples, the death of the one is followed often and usually soon by the death of the other. They cannot, literally, live without each other; and the death of the survivor seems neither accident nor coincidence. That this mysterious mechanism of will exists in many of us, consciously or subconsciously, deserves far more attention than it has so far been given.

I believe that the will to die is the direct reflection of the quality of life. And if that quality is indeed being debased by the mounting brutality, boredom, fragmentation, and frustration that mark our society, then the conscious choice in the very ill or severely maimed or old for a "good death," is a wholly valid one, to be honored by us all, including the doctors empowered to help them achieve it.

VIII
The Big Questions

1. SUICIDE

These are all actual cases, although for obvious reasons their names and initials are changed.

1. Responding to an emergency call, Dr. Y. found himself faced with the following situation. The patient was an unconscious lawyer, who apparently had ingested twenty capsules of Nembutal prescribed for him the previous day. Attached to the top of his pajamas was the following letter:

Dear Doctor:

As you know, you are not allowed to treat a patient without his consent. In most cases an implied consent is all which is needed. When the patient arrives at the doctor's office or the doctor is called to the patient's bedside, it is implied that the patient agrees to be treated. In surgical cases, the surgeon will ask for a written informed consent to a specific procedure.

In the case of an unconscious patient, it is usually assumed that the patient would give his consent for treatment if his unconsciousness would not prevent him from doing so. In my case such assumption would be erroneous. I am of absolutely sound mind. To prove it, I underwent extensive psychiatric examinations, and attached to this letter you will find a notarized statement from my psychiatrist attesting to my absolutely sound mind and complete mental health. My intention to commit suicide is not caused by any mental disturbance, but by my wish to escape a lingering demise in my desperate physical condition (carcinomatosis of the spine and spinal cord and gangrenous decubital ulcers).

I do not give consent to treatment. On the contrary, I herewith interdict any treatment aimed at my regaining consciousness or prolonging my life. Anyone who might act against my order of refraining from any life-prolonging procedures will personally be held responsible for his acts, including financial responsibility, which because of hospitalization for possibly much longer than a year, may run into substantial amounts.

A copy of this letter will be found in my safe-deposit box.

A. Y.
Attorney at Law

The psychiatrist who sent me a Xerox of this statement added: How should a doctor act in such a situation? Withhold treatment or prolong his suffering?

2. Mary, a sixty-year-old friend of mine with an impeccable life of service to humanity and kindness to others, called in distress one day about a certain request made of her.

The evening before she had visited Anne, her close friend of decades, who was now in her eighties, blind, and paralyzed after a long and distinguished career as an archeologist and professor. She lived with a full-time nurse in her own small apartment, confined to a wheelchair and unable to perform her functions without help.

Far worse, for her, she could not of course read or see the beauties of form and color and texture either of the antiquity she cherished nor of the natural world her love of country living had always afforded her. She had no close relations: they had all died.

Mary told me that while the nurse was out of the room that evening, she had whispered to her, "Please, please, help me to die. I don't want to live anymore. . . . I want to die. But I don't know how. Please, please, tell me how."

In deep distress and compassion, Mary told her she didn't know how but would make every effort to find a way. She herself never took pills for anything, being one of those sturdy souls who believe that taking aspirin for a pain is a sign of weakness.

When she got home, she said, she called a close social worker friend with some medical training and asked her advice. Joan said she could see only one way to help: tell her own—Mary's—doctor that she was going through a long spell of insomnia and needed barbiturates (Joan named several brands) to get her back into the patterns of sleep. On the assumption—and particularly because of Mary's long record of nonaddiction to anything—that he would give her a prescription, the next step would be remove the label from the drugstore container, bring the pills to her desperate friend on her next visit, and tell her to take them all.

"I'm calling you," Mary said to me, "because I don't know whether I can or should actually go ahead with it."

I said I understood the extent of her responsibility, but if the situation was as virtually hopeless as she described it, and Anne in great need, I myself would provide these measures. Mary sighed deeply over the phone, thanked me, and hung up.

I never asked her what happened then, nor have I seen Anne's obituary ("died suddenly in her sleep"?) in the papers.

It is possible that Mary simply could not bring herself to take these steps, or that the nurse somehow prevented the pills from reaching her patient.

Were Mary and Joan and I conspirators in murder? Would the doctor or nurse or any one of us want to live Anne's despairing life?

———

Paradoxes have formed the core of all our thinking in terms of suicide, as in euthanasia. We continue to call suicide "irrational" on the extraordinary assumption that the millions of people in this world who continue to lead miserable lives are "rational."

But then David Hume in his essay on suicide in 1777 crystallized the issue for medical ethics by asserting that if our shortening lives interferes with Providence, then medical services are already interfering by lengthening them.

According to the *Codex Iuris* of Canada, "This double standard is now a part of our established mores or customary morality. We are, by some strange habit of mind and heart, willing to impose death but un-willing to permit it: we will justify humanly contrived death when it violates the human integrity of its vic-tims, but we condemn it when it is an intelligent vol-untary decision. If death is not inevitable anyway, not desired by the subject, and not merciful, it is righteous! If it is happening anyway, and is freely embraced and merciful, then it is wrong!"

We may also remember that the early Church con-demned the taking of life in military service, and yet it finally consented to it when a political concordat became a strong enough inducement.

It was this kind of thinking that made the end of Jonathan Swift's life such unremitting physical and spiritual agony. According to Richard Garnett's biog-raphy of the great satirist, he was so demoralized with, among other tortures, the acute pain in his eye that knives had to be kept out of his reach as were the deadly drugs he craved. "He wanted to commit what the law calls suicide and what vitalist ethics calls sin. Standing by was some good doctor of physick, trem-bling with sympathy and frustration. Secretly, perhaps, he wanted to commit what the law calls murder. Both had full knowledge of the way out, which is half the foundation of moral integrity, but unlike his patient the physician felt he had no freedom to act, which is the other half of moral integrity."

For his last three years, Swift sat and drooled, and at least five years before he died in fits of convulsion lasting thirty-six hours, he had written to his niece: "I am so stupid and confounded that I cannot express the mortification I am under both of body and soul."

Garnett concludes: "The story of this man's death points us directly to the broad problem of suicide, as well as to the more particular problem of euthanasia.

We get a glimpse of this paradox in our present customary morality, that it sometimes condemns us to live, or, to put it another way, destroys our moral being for the sake of just *being.*"

There is also a common ambivalence in the attitude that suicide is a form of cowardice. To evade self requires no courage: to face self and perform the act of consciously destroying it demands great courage. No reversal is possible.

And if aiding and abetting suicide is a crime, then mercy and compassion are both crimes. And the men who withheld the knife and the drug from the raging Jonathan Swift are heroes and saints.

2. THE UNWILLED

Those who so passionately uphold the "sanctity of life" do not ask "what life?" nor see themselves as retarded and crippled in an institution for the rest of that life. Nor do they choose to see, or think of, the tens of thousands of lives born crippled and retarded, who, without will or choice, were allowed to be born as, presumably, the "right" of the damaged fetus *to* life.

Rather than seeing the many tangible horrors of that life, the sanctity people choose to emphasize the maternal love and care transcending the agony of a malformed or mindless presence, day after day and year after year. Or they point to those few institutions where a dedicated staff and the latest therapies bring these children or adults to a minimal level of competence: dressing themselves, cleaning themselves, learning small tasks. Since these "inmates" sometimes play and sometimes smile, they are, of course, "happy." They know no other existence, they act on reflexes, not will.

Certainly, love is the prime need of these incomplete beings, whether born that way or the victims of violent and crippling accident. Two middle-aged couples I know who cannot give such grown sons or daughters the special help they need, visit them where they live every week, stay with them for hours. "Ben is such a beautiful young man," said one father. "It's still hard to believe that his fine face and body can exist without thought processes or directions. The circuits in his brain just don't connect."

Certainly, there are parents who love their mongoloid and retarded children, accept them with their siblings as part of the family. But the "sanctity of life" people forget what an enormous toll it takes of the mother especially, who bore this child before the relatively new science of fetology could have given her the alternative choice: not to bear a permanently deformed or retarded being. For it has now become possible, with extremely delicate instruments and techniques, to establish deformation and brain damage, among other serious handicaps, in the unborn fetus when suspicions of malfunctioning exist.

Yet to the antiabortionists, any birth is presumably better than no birth. They seem to forget that millions of unwanted children all over this world are not only destined for an uncherished and mean existence, but swell a population already threatening the resources of this planet, let alone its bare amenities.

They also choose to ignore the kind of "homes" in every large community where the pitiful accidents of biology sit half-naked on floors strewn with feces, autistic and motionless, or banging their swollen heads against peeling walls.

If the concept of "sanctity" does not include "quality," then the word has no meaning and less humanity. The rights of birth and death, of life itself, require both.

Above all, how can the sanctity-of-life argument prevail in a society that condones death in war of young men who want to live, but will not permit the old and hopelessly ill, craving release, to die?

3. MERCY KILLING

Once more, the interweaving of notes and phrases in this complex oratorio of death brings euthanasia and mercy killing together—echoes and conjunctions. Euthanasia concerns the desire of one person to cease living and the act of one doctor to permit death in circumstances of incurable suffering or terminal disease. Mercy killing is the conscious act of one person toward another, of any age, performed to spare the other from an intolerable life.

The classic mercy killing of our time occurred in the early fifties and was widely reported in the press far beyond the New England town where it happened. One account written by Dean Sperry of the Harvard Divinity School touched the salient points of the case:

A country doctor in New Hampshire, Dr. Herman N. Sander, was arrested on the charge of murder. He had had as a patient in the Hillsboro County Hospital a fifty-nine-year-old woman who was dying of cancer. She had wasted from 140 pound to 80 pounds. The end was inevitable and very near. Torn with pity for her suffering he had given her in a vein four lethal injections of air, 10 cubic centimeters each. The frothy blood that resulted formed an embolus of which she died within ten minutes. He then entered on the hospital records an account of what he had done, and let the matter rest there.

The heads of the hospital, going over the case records

of the patients at a staff meeting, came across this entry and reported it to the state. A warrant for the doctor's arrest was issued and served by the sheriff, charging that Dr. Sander "feloniously and willfully and of his own malice aforethought did inject . . . air into the veins of Abbie Borroto, and with said air injection, feloniously, willfully and of his said malice aforethought killed and murdered" his patient. The doctor pleaded not guilty, was released on twenty-five thousand dollars bail, and bound over for a hearing before the grand jury. Two days later, the grand jury remanded him for trial.

All reports indicated that Dr. Sander was a trusted and honored practitioner. His father had been an official of the Public Service Corporation of New Hampshire. As an undergraduate, he had captained the ski team at Dartmouth during his college days and had been a member of the college symphony orchestra. He had recently returned from a trip to Europe, where he had been studying socialized medicine, and was scheduled for a number of lectures on the subject. There was no question of any prior illegality in his practice, and his record was above reproach.

As for his act on this occasion, he said that he had done no wrong. The woman was within hours of her death. Prompted by pity, he had merely hastened what would have been the end in any case. On the Sunday after his arrest, he went with his family to the Congregational Church in Candia, as was his custom. His minister publicly expressed sympathy for him, while the minister of the First Congregational Church in the nearby city of Manchester preached a stirring sermon in his defense. The latter clergyman said that if the doctor was guilty, he too was guilty: for he had often prayed that some suffering parishioner might be "eased into the experience of death." Later in the day, 605 of the 650 registered voters in the town of Candia presented Dr. Sander with an unqualified testimonial as to his integrity and good name, telling him to use it hereafter as he might see fit.

Meanwhile, the attorney-general of New Hampshire, who was Dr. Sander's personal friend, said that "the case will be presented forcefully and in complete detail, regardless of personalities and theories involved, to the end that justice may be met." At the time of writing it was impossible to tell what the result of the ensuing trial would be.

The whole affair brought the arguments of mercy killing to a head. The Euthanasia Society of America had been agitating over some years for a change in the laws, to allow mercy killing. They suggested that such killing had been tacitly practiced by many physicians and that this irregular practice, which they held to be desirable and morally defensible, should be legally regularized. An officer of the society visited New Hampshire and said that they regarded this incident as a concrete example of the need for euthanasia. They hoped that the State of New Hampshire might, as a result, legalize mercy killing.

According to Dr. Sperry, the act of Dr. Sander conformed in theory to the program proposed by the Euthanasia Society. "Dr. Sander differed from the Society mainly in this, that he took the law into his own hands and went ahead on his own account. The nurse who had handed him the syringe that he used apparently had no knowledge of what he was doing and was cleared of any suspicion of being *particeps criminis*. Had he not duly entered the transaction on the hospital records he would probably have gone scot free. One can only con-

clude that, in making the entry after the act, he deliber-
ately intended to make of his private act a public test
case."

This Dr. Sander most certainly did. Had he not dic-
tated notes for the case record to Miss Josephine Connor, the record librarian at the county hospital, and had
Miss Connor not touched off the investigation, Sander
would never been brought to trial.

And although hundreds of his fellow townspeople,
his patients, and his colleagues offered to testify on his
behalf and signed petitions urging the courts to dismiss
his case, a grand jury indicted him for first-degree murder. "All that I can say," said Sander, "is that I am not
guilty of any legal or moral wrong and ultimately my
position will be vindicated."

It was; and not long afterward he was acquitted.
Although his license to practice was temporarily suspended and certain pastors fulminated against him
from their pulpits—among them the Reverend Billy
Graham, who said in Boston that "Dr. Sander should be
punished as an example" and that "anyone who volun-
tarily, knowingly or premeditatedly takes the life of
another, even one minute prior to death, is a killer"—
most public sentiment was for him. (So have most
juries, presented with similar cases, rendered "not
guilty" verdicts.)

After he had supported himself and his family for a
period as a farmhand for four dollars an hour, the
Medical Board of the State of New Hampshire eventually reinstated his license, and he has since spent
peaceful years of practice in his home town.

Even so, and even now, there is nowhere in the common law any toleration for mercy killing. The condemn-
ing thunder of Blackstone, deity-father of common law

and hence of the body of most of our inherited statutes, rolls on, whether euthanasia, abortion, suicide, or mercy killing is in question.

Speaking of accessories to suicide, he observes: "The law in such cases can only reach the man's reputation and fortune. Hence, it has ordered an ignominious burial in the highway with a stake driven through the offender's body and the forfeiture of his goods and chattels to the king."

Thus, through the wisdom and mercy of God, was the sanctity of life sustained—in the eyes of the righteous.

In the eyes of the just, on the other hand, one would be more inclined to echo the words of one Roman citizen reacting to a famous mercy killing some years ago in his city. "It would have to happen to you before you could know what to do."

This concerned a young father who dropped his deformed infant son from a bridge to his death in the Tiber River.

The baby, Ivano, was born without legs or fingers. The twenty-nine-year-old father, Livio Davani, was in jail on a charge of murder. The minimum penalty was ten years in prison.

"My son would never have forgiven me if I had let him live only to suffer," Davani told police when he gave himself up.

Out of one hundred Romans interviewed by the capital's independent newspaper, *Il Messaggero*, twenty-two said they would have done what the father did; thirty-one said they would not; forty-seven did not know.

Davani, a photoengraver, had gone to San Camillo Hospital and taken out his son, born twenty-eight days earlier. For four hours he drove through the streets.

Then he stopped his car and carried the baby halfway across the Flaminian Bridge.

" 'I took off his little dress,' the father was quoted as saying, 'and saw again how he was deformed. He began crying, because it was time for his bottle. I could no longer resist. Grown, he would have cursed me. I don't care how long they keep me in prison. Now I am more serene.'

"His wife, Nada, who talked with him half an hour in jail, said she would appeal to President Giuseppe Saragat for clemency. 'He is not an assassin,' she said. 'He did it for the baby. He could not let it suffer.' Prosecutor Mario Schiavotti, charging Davani with willful homicide, said, 'It's tragic but that's the law. What can I do?' "

The defense attorney, one of Italy's leading criminal lawyers, planned to contend that Davani acted under irresistible emotional strain, and the Vatican newspaper *L'Osservatore Romano* commented that "evidently the father was the victim of psychological shock which demands tremendous compassion." But it added: "Human life is a gift of which God is the supreme judge and of which only He can dispose."

Would the Vatican writer has wanted to live his life without legs or fingers? It would seem that strict adherence to faith can at one and the same time provide personal solace, yet also a shield against that empathy which permits one to suffer what others suffer and understand why they do what they must do.

The quality of mercy cannot be strained when mercy inspires the act under judgment. And when the law and the Church can find no distinction between good and evil intent, they have abdicated their service to humanity.

Now, here in America, this distinction has become vital, whether the object of "mercy killing" or active euthanasia is a deformed and mindless infant or the human wreckage of a car crash, multiple fractures and concussion leading to irreversible coma. Whether the one who ends this half-life is a doctor or a parent or a loving friend, the inherent mercy of such an act should weigh heavily in its favor where legal or moral judgment is concerned.

Since God cannot dispose of these "gifts of life" which have turned to curses, then man will have to.

IX
The Evolving Church

Since belief in a Supreme Being, creator of the cosmos, of earth, of man and all living beings is the cornerstone of the great religions, the simple phrase "The Lord giveth, the Lord taketh away" is still the prime source of opposition. Suicide, contraception, anesthesia, cremation, abortion, even divorce: all these have in turn been construed by religious orthodoxy as offenses against the divine—hence natural—order, and as a sin against the Holy Spirit.

But during the same long years and against the same harsh strictures, single voices—even among the faithful—have been raised in defense of acts of love and compassion that have also formed the basis of Catholic, Protestant, and Judaic theology. These will be heard more and more in coming months and pages.

As a notable nonbeliever, Bertrand Russell wrote in *Why I Am Not a Christian*, in the late fifties, "Collective wisdom, alas, is no adequate substitute for the intelligence of individuals. Individuals who opposed received opinions have have been the source of all progress, both moral and intellectual. They have been unpopular, as was natural. Socrates, Christ, and Galileo all equally incurred the censure of the orthodox."

It is not so easy now, in democratic societies, to silence rebels, although the chill of political thought-control began—after twenty years—to pervade the flow of free information and expression in this country. Since it had already impeded action on population control (the commission report that gave it high priority was virtually tabled), and since state governments (with a White House nod and religious pressures) were about to reverse a national trend toward liberalized abortion before the recent Supreme Court decision upheld women's rights to privacy in this matter, opposition to euthanasia may temporarily harden.

It provides some comfort then, to know that the Reformed Church of the Netherlands has issue a report on euthanasia that has opened the door wide for free and untrammeled consideration of what it clearly considers a vital human issue.

This report, passed unanimously by the General Synod in February of 1972, is one of the most temperate and enlightened statements ever made by an important religious body.

It defines the difference between passive and active euthanasia, admits the difficulty of drawing a line between them, and yet concedes one notable distinction: that of doing nothing or doing something.

It notes that with the advance in medical science, serious ethical problems have confronted doctors, who—along with a committee of theologians and ethicians—had made repeated requests of the Church to clarify them.

The report opens with a general survey of euthanasia's

part in that tenuous area where life ends and death starts, and then deals specifically with the doctor and the dying patient, the severely deformed born baby, victims of road accidents, the aged and chronic patient, the patient's own responsibility, and suicide as a form of euthanasia.

Most importantly, the Synod said that one looks in vain to the Bible for well-defined guidelines for man's ethical behavior, since issues that now demand our attention were then unknown.

The Synod does stress, however, that death, as life, should be endowed with meaning, and that cases of *indirect* euthanasia that may shorten life as the result of humane objectives, can be fully justified.

". . . When the boundary of no-man's land between life and death has been crossed, then the patient stops being a historic man with an individuality of his own and with the ability of contacting, at some future time, the outside world . . . then further medical treatment may be stopped, just as it may be equally justified not to start with a medical treatment if the prognosis leaves no doubt of reaching any result."

The Synod clearly—and boldly—does not believe surgical intervention is justified in cases of children born severely deformed and incapable of living a communicative life. Nor should medical science lengthen the lives, against their wish, of those elderly persons who are "satiated with what life has to offer."

The Synod believes that because so large an amount of energy and medicine is used for the incurably ill, a choice has to be made, and the question asked: "Is there a limit to what has to be done for only a few?"

The report acknowledges opposing arguments, but counters that God made men responsible for the choice whether to procreate or not, and whether to put an end to life or not. They need not necessarily wait passively for death to come.

The Synod comes out strongly for close cooperation between doctor, nursing staff, and pastor, in guiding the seriously ill in the process of dying as an important phase in their lives.

The report never diminishes the importance of faith in Jesus Christ and God's faithfulness in living and in dying, but it says that the pastorate must be concerned equally with people in other situations of adversity and with possible lack of faith.

The tone of this report is as moderate as its content is revolutionary, in terms of liberation from dogma, from the automatic reflexes of entrenched religious hierarchies.

It may, in fact, be called a new kind of "collective wisdom"; the product of a time in history when those who belong to an established social, political, or religious institution begin to question their validity—at least in part—in the light of immense and often convulsive change.

It has taken Catholics a long time to reassess their traditional views on birth control, waging fierce battles against contraception and fiercer ones against abortion. Yet these have not prevented a growing number of their flock from resorting to both; and Catholics aware of the changing tide may have to temper their opposition to euthanasia.

One such Catholic conceded four years ago that "we ought to be able to recognize the possibility, at least, that those of our contemporaries who are concerned to discuss all aspects of 'death control' are not necessarily a group of potential murderers intent on the further diminishment of man."

They might remember too that St. Augustine in his

Confessions, pleaded for a keener awareness of death, not to dull the thirst for life but to intensify the self's awareness of life.

Nor can Catholics overlook what Pope Pius XII said in 1957 to the International Congress of Anesthesiologists: that although the physician has the obligation to use all ordinary means of preserving life, there is no absolute obligation to use extraordinary means.

That the Pope then defined euthanasia unlawful as "the direct disposing of the life of the patient," in no way diminished the prior implication that even the "sanctity of life" had its limits, regardless of whether medical science could extend it.

And Jewish attitudes? Boiled down from the monumental *Talmudic Encyclopedia*, they indicate clearly that any form of *active* euthanasia is strictly prohibited and condemned as plain murder, and that anyone who kills a dying person is liable to the death penalty as a common murderer. At the same time, Jewish law sanctions the withdrawal of any factor—whether extraneous to the patient or not—which may artificially delay his demise in the *final* phase.

All such strictures or permissions, in Jewish law, refer to an individual in whom death is expected to be imminent—three days or less in Rabbinic references.

This means that passive euthanasia in a patient who may yet live (in whatever condition) for weeks or months may not be condoned.

There are increasing numbers of unorthodox Jews, however, who have not only come out openly for euthanasia in circumstances that warrant it, but who, as Jewish theologians, doctors, social workers, and writers, are vocal supporters of passive, if not active, euthanasia as inherently just and humane in specific circumstances.

So we are now faced—believers and atheists alike—with profound and critical choices at both ends of the human span. Whether to be born as a whole and wanted human being, or without love or health. Whether to die with dignity and by desire, or with neither will nor choice in the manner of dying.

In both cases, God's will is as ambiguous as "Thou shalt not kill," since religious zeal has occasioned the bloodiest wars in history, and since divine will has heaped unspeakable torments on saint and sinner alike.

Might it be that because of this "blessing" of suffering, more and more human beings are turning to Christ instead as the fount of compassion; a man "acquainted with grief"? And that the Supreme Being is losing His power as mortals are discovering theirs?

In so doing they are forfeiting the luxuries of impotence. They can no longer accept poverty, disease, injustice, or war as God's will, exempting them of responsibility or decision. They can no longer hope for answers to prayer, for forgiveness for sin, for rewards in heaven. They can no longer comfort themselves with immortality except in the hearts of the living.

What the best of them can do, by their own efforts and sacrifice, is to make human society profoundly humane. Only through love and enlightenment can this come about: the education of the spirit, of the mind, and of the body toward their ultimate reach.

We will then achieve a collective conscience that will accept any change found essential toward such ends, and repudiate any power designed to curtail and diminish them.

That this humane society will be long in coming needs no saying, since among its requirements are a long period of peace, profound changes in education, and a massive reorganization of priorities in the task of saving this planet and its peoples. New political systems will have to emerge that will transcend national interests in favor of universal needs, and new leaders trained to innovate and preside over their fulfillment.

In the case of priorities, death has now at least emerged as a major one, since it claims us all. And all the religious, political, and social forces in the world can no longer silence the single voices and proliferating groups who insist on an open dialogue and concerted action toward insuring the final rights of those who claim them.

X
The Rising Chorus

In the last thirty years more and more single voices of prominent citizens have been raised in the United States and Great Britain in support not only of their own beliefs but of those groups in both countries devoted to spreading the concept of euthanasia.

The Euthanasia Society in London was founded in 1935; the American Euthanasia Society, incorporating the Euthanasia Educational Fund, emerged three years later. And in May of 1973, the Netherlands formed its Euthanasia Society.

In 1968 the two joined forces when the American society held a conference in New York. The principal speaker was Sir George Thomson, Nobel Laureate in physics, formerly master of Corpus Christi College in Cambridge University, and vice president of the British group.

In his speech he said that our respective societies "in their early days derived their greatest emotional drive from the desire to save from unnecessary pain those who were certainly dying, especially from cancer." He concedes that there has been some improvement here, though not enough. Yet since a certain court judgment in 1957, it was generally agreed that a doctor was entitled to use enough drugs to deaden pain in a case that was certain to end fatally, even though to do so would hasten death.

He remarked that although the doctor is not obliged to do so, probably most do; and that one of the new clauses the British society hoped to put forward was to make it quite certain that the patient is entitled to this treatment if he asks for it.

But the great physicist was chiefly concerned with the consequences of modern medicine in keeping alive patients who have little or no chance of recovery.

"Why should people be obliged to live unwillingly for an indefinite period in a state which is a travesty of humanity, retaining only its most sordid elements . . . ?"

He said that since 1961 suicide was no longer a crime in Britain, though "by a magnificent illogicality," it was punishable to be an accomplice of suicide.

Sir George conceded that circumstances could exist in which the "accomplice" might be exerting unjustifiable pressure for selfish reasons, but the fact that regulations were indicated did not warrant forbidding the practice entirely. "One does not ban automobiles because speed-limits are sometimes needed."

Speaking at the same conference was a journalist and author who had been among the first to raise the euthanasia-suicide issue in this country, Lael Wertenbaker. In 1947, her book called *Death of a Man* described in often agonizing detail the mutually planned death of her husband Charles Wertenbaker, then foreign editor of *Time*.

Twenty years later she began her talk at this conference by confessing that she had never made up her mind as to exactly what legal forms euthanasia should take because as a foreign correspondent in Berlin she had learned too much about what the Nazis had done, and therefore was as concerned with *protection* against abuse as deeply as with the problem itself. Yet when her husband received his sentence of death by cancer, "we faced two problems which are germane. The first . . . is the necessity to live with the awareness of death, and the second is the right to truth. I have found that there are far more people who do want the truth and would continue to face the truth as Charles Wertenbaker did than are given this opportunity, or given the right to live as my husband and I did in the perspective of death, which is an extraordinary perspective and a quite brilliantly clarifying one.

"We are now dealing with the suffering of the body which does not affect the mind. In this, in living with him, in directly facing it together, using the words and understanding of the fact that death was inevitable— and imminent—we had the most enormous reward."

Lael Wertenbaker made it clear that although what they did was technically suicide—his will, her aiding and abetting—it was in no way rejection of life, which he loved. "It was a *choosing of the moment*, it was the cup of hemlock when you are already under sentence of death."

In her highly controversial book, the process began with increasing doses of morphine (increasingly difficult to obtain), and ended with cutting the arteries of the wrist. Since they could get no medical help, they were forced to such measures.

But as the mother of two children, her main thrust at this conference was toward the education of the young in the matter of death and dying. "I think one of our great problems is the failure to speak of, to accept and to acknowledge death from the time we are very young. . . . one reason why people do not wish to be told the truth by doctors and doctors are afraid to tell the truth, is because they have not faced it all along, but only at the end."

In the discussion that followed, a woman described her experience with her dying husband, a chemist. "He had all the treatment and everything that was possible, with which he cooperated. The time came when he should die and I stood by while he took cyanide. I am glad I did it and proud of him for having the courage to do it."

During these interchanges of opinion, the entirely voluntary aspects of self-imposed death were repeatedly stressed. "In my opinion," said the physicist, "the individual is the best judge of how long his death should be held back. . . . If he has left nothing in writing and is unable to communicate them, his views as expressed in health should be given careful consideration and weight."

Four years after this ground-breaking conference, a public figure of political prominence raised his voice at a conference in Dorchester, Massachusetts: Governor McCall of Oregon.

"What I am talking about," he said, "is death with dignity, in one's advanced years, as opposed to death as a vegetable." He described this as a conscious decision to refrain from life-supporting machines and medicine that merely prolonged the suffering and degradation of the deathbed.

"A very important part of my constituency," said the governor, "has asked me to take leadership on this issue."

The governor has, bringing up all the troubling questions so long unaired, so long avoided; considering a possible amendment to the state constitution, answering emotional attacks with consistent reason. "To imply that a governor cannot even bring up the subject is unthinkable, especially to a governor whose life as newsman and public official has revolved around creating and stimulating dialogue on the great issues, regardless of their volatility."

And when Governor McCall met with his Oregon delegates at the White House Conference on Aging, one of their highest priority recommendations was "The right to die with dignity [to be] recognized by religious bodies and government."

One of the Oregon governor's allies in thinking is Dr. Walter W. Sackett, Jr., a general practitioner in Miami and a member of the Florida House of Representatives. In 1968 he proposed an amendment to the Basic Rights Article of the Constitution of the State of Florida, which read as follows:

"All natural persons are equal before the law and have inalienable rights, among which are the right to enjoy and defend life, liberty, *to be permitted to die with dignity*, to pursue happiness . . ." and ending, "No person shall be deprived of any right because of race or religion."

A year later, Dr. Sackett explained his views in detail, remarking that opposition to his amendment came "strangely enough" more from his own medical community than from any other single group.

Although assured of substantial support from powerful colleagues, his bill was swiftly defeated. Sackett was therefore hardly prepared, he wrote, for the kindly words of his fellow legislators, at least twenty-five of whom gave him encouragement and urged him to bring the matter up again in an off-election year.

The bulk of his mail, however, was overwhelmingly supportive of his position, and almost every major newspaper in the state carried a favorable editorial or a noncritical commentary on the proposed amendment.

After describing several instances of prolonged and agonizing death, Dr. Sackett writes, "To me, there is no rule of conscience, no dogma of religion, and no law of sovereign authority that permits a philosophy of perpetuation of meaningless life. All such forces should dictate to the contrary."

It is significant that Dr. Sackett is a Catholic physician, challenged by bishops and other members of the clergy concerning his views. He reminds them that the Pope (Paul VI) stated "that heroic measures are not indicated in hopeless situations."

Sackett ends by remarking that during legislative proceedings, both in the committee and on the floor, comment is often made that a certain piece of legislation is needed, but that the public is not ready and must, therefore, be educated to its importance and necessity.

"Here," he concludes, "is a situation wherein the reverse is true. The public *is* ready for this amendment."

Ready or not, Dr. Sackett has proposed his "death with dignity" bill in his state's legislature every year since 1968. It finally passed the House on May 25, 1973, by a close vote, and was sent to the Senate with the approval of the Health and Rehabilitation Services Committee.

In the international arena, moves were made six years ago by the then Secretary General U Thant to incorporate euthanasia and allied subjects in the field of human rights. One of them concerned the decision as to when the donor was dead before the removal of a vital organ for transplant. Although the end of the heartbeat had for long been considered the final signal, the newer concept of "brain death" had become the accepted determinant.

The report raised a.) "the risk of living donors in transplant operations, viewed in the light of the likely benefit in each operation."

b.) The question of free consent as applied to living donors in transplant operations.

c.) The right to life as applied to donors in transplant operations that a donor cannot survive, viewed in the light of new medical definitions of death.

d.) The dignity of a human being, viewed in the light of the existence of techniques for the artificial prolongation of certain bodily functions after the cerebral function has ceased.

These medical questions were part of a 151-page report on human rights and modern science on order of the General Assembly in a resolution dated December 19, 1968, the result of recommendations by the International Conference on Human Rights in Teheran that year.

Since then, medical science has advanced, answering some of the questions but by no means all. And least of all, the dignity of dying. The voices of those demanding this human right still remain silent . . . or the legislators do not choose to hear them when they do speak.

XI
Should There Be a Law?

In a medical-legal reader published in 1956 and mainly concerned with medical science and crime, and laws regulating medicine, the word *euthanasia* is neither in text nor index, although laws against mercy killing—sometimes, and erroneously, applied to euthanasia—exist in all our states.

Suicide is no longer a criminal offense in this country, nor in England; although anyone aiding and abetting suicide is liable to a charge of murder here, and of manslaughter there.

Euthanasia per se does not exist in the statutes of France or Belgium, although considered as premeditated homicide. However, a bill to legalize euthanasia for some "damaged" children came before the Belgian government in 1962 following the famous Liège trial involving parents, relatives, and a physician charged with murdering a Thalidomide-damaged child.

In Italy, euthanasia is a crime only if the victim is under eighteen years of age, mentally retarded, or "menaced under the effect of fear." More tolerant attitudes prevail also in Denmark, Holland, Yugoslavia, and even Catholic Spain.

Switzerland seems to have the most lenient legislation. Revamped in 1951, the Swiss penal code distinguishes between killing with bad intentions, i.e., murder, and killing with good intentions, that is, euthanasia. In Sweden, passive euthanasia was legalized in 1964.

Legislating morality is at best a dubious exercise, at worst an invasion of individual rights. Only in deterrence of the killing and harming of others for gain, for revenge, for power or for self-gratification can laws hope to humanize man. Judging from the state of our own society now, they have been largely impotent even there.

Our prisons grow fuller and fuller, breeding more criminals, our bombs have killed millions of strangers in a merciless rain, and no man or woman can walk a city expecting safety. Sadism is mass entertainment, hate is public nutrition.

It would seem wiser, therefore, to make no laws curtailing or penalizing the very basic human rights of self-preservation or self-destruction when neither infringes on the rights of others. At a time when wanton and violent death is a daily fact, any law against the good and peaceful death, euthanasia, would seem a farce.

It would certainly be of no help to doctor, dying patient, or family. Like love and creation, dying is a private matter.

To argue against this compassion, moreover, in a world where violence and brutality have become epidemic in even "advanced" societies such as ours, to distrust the motives of compassionate acts, merely spreads the contagion.

Yet the assumption that no civilized society can exist without laws still holds firm. One can still argue about what *civilized* means, and whether indeed we qualify for the term. We can also point to primitive societies that survived as tribal entities in relative order merely through unwritten taboos.

But laws are tricky. They are particularly tricky when they enter the domain of private relationships at a moment in history where drastic changes in social mores have made many laws concerned with morality ineffectual, ambiguous, or obsolete.

For the efficacy of laws depends not on the lawmakers but on the nature of the citizenry to which they apply. The body of laws incorporated from English common law in our constitution assumed, in this new small nation, a citizenry not unlike the men who devised it and signed it. The first Americans were largely of British stock, literate if not all well educated, land owners (if not African slaves), by nature respectful of laws and their enforcers. Even the nonconformists who left their own land and Church to acquire freedom of belief, believed in the Ten Commandments, of which "Thou shalt not kill" and "Thou shalt not steal" have been held incontrovertible except in war and the spoils of war.

For the majority of our citizens, perhaps they still speak to the conscience, restraining them from murder and felony. For an ever-growing minority, however, fear of arrest and punishment, however severe short of death, has failed to inhibit acts of violence, from gratuitous and unpremeditated murder to armed assault and robbery. Laws have not stopped sick assassins from killing Presidents, nor teen-age boys from mugging and stealing at random. Long racial oppression and poverty have been held responsible for much of this crime, with the dope habit a major and coexistent factor. The tendency among sociologists and psychologists in particular is to find excuses for widespread vandalism, bombing of property, and "ripping off"—if not killing itself—in social or political terms as acts against the money establishment, the corporate powers, the repressive machinery of "law and order."

To be sure, the offenders (when found) are arrested, given prison terms, or—in hundreds of instances—let loose on the streets the next day or the next year; back to do what they did before.

In the private or personal sector, punitive laws against abortion have not prevented hundreds of thousands of women from having them, nor have the penalties for adultery in certain states in any manner decreased illicit relationships or increasing sexual freedom, including what used to be called "unnatural acts" or "sexual deviation."

There is a strong argument to be made against any law, therefore, defining or impinging upon the manner in which men and women choose to live—or die. Any law, in short, designed to define and punish evil motives in the performance of euthanasia, passive or active, would implicitly bring good motives into question as well. And the persons who, even at the explicit request of the patient in question, acceded to it, would have to answer in court for an act of mercy. This is why many, if by no means all, ardent supporters of euthanasia doubt the value, at this particular point, of a law permitting it on certain condition, and requiring both evidence and testimony from those committing it.

Of those who would favor such a law, most would consider it an essential protection for the doctors and staff involved in this act, on whatever grounds of mercy (subject, of course, to proof), and—even more—as a protection against those practicing euthanasia for evil motives in the name of national good.

The argument here would seem potent. It is, in effect, that once you are sanctioned to kill the terminally ill or dying in our population (even by their express will), there is nothing to stop you from killing a wide range of other social "burdens": the defective, the deformed, the retarded, the insane, experimental human guinea pigs, and so forth. It would be a vast form of *triage*, a term used by medical teams on battlefields to treat first those wounded combatants with the clear chance of survival, and leave the most gravely injured, the most likely to die, to the last.

This would presuppose a wholly savage society, on Nazi lines, or one so mercilessly money-oriented that we could take a crushing load off our national budget by removing the unproductive and unfit: the expense of caring for society's rejects and genetic accidents is, the argument could claim, prodigious.

There are plenty of people, in fact, who include expulsion of the fetus through abortion in this list, and equate it with murder; as if the fetus were a living human being with will and conscience—a profoundly questionable assumption at the very least.

The express will of the seriously afflicted patient is then, as always, the determining factor in the good or bad motives involved in hastening death when life barely exists as it is.

It would seem then, that what is needed is not so much a new statute on the books but a legal validation of the patient's written request for euthanasia: a request defining the circumstances, complete and detailed, mental and physical, in which the time for this release is desired.

XII
The Creative Spirit

I died for beauty, but was scarce
Adjusted in the tomb,
When one who died for truth was lain
In an adjoining room.

He questioned softly why I failed?
"For beauty," I replied.
"And I for truth,—the two are one;
We brethren are," he said.

And so, as kinsmen met a night,
We talked between the rooms,
Until the moss had reached our lips,
And covered up our names.

Emily Dickinson

It should come as no surprise that those who give us the most profound insights into death are those who have most fully lived the life of the spirit: the creators among us.

That is why I have chosen here not only to use their own words, in prose or verse, but to show the few available masks of great human beings, made of their features in death. Both indicate, at least to this writer, a kind of transcendence not necessarily confined to the great among us, the sublimely gifted, but apparent also in the faces of the humble and unrecorded after life has left them. Conspicuous among these is the young unknown "suicide of the Seine" shown here.

One of the wisest comments on the phenomenon of the creator and death is this passage by J. W. N. Sullivan, the musicologist, in a book on Beethoven, published in 1927.

> *The great artist achieves a relative immortality because the experiences he deals with are as fundamental for humanity as are hunger, sex, and the succession of day and night. It does not follow that the experiences he communicates are elementary. They may belong to an order of consciousness that very few men have attained, but, in that case, they must be in the line of human development; we must feel them as prophetic.*
>
> *Beethoven's late music communicates experiences that very few people can normally possess. . . . They correspond to a spiritual synthesis which the race has not achieved but which, we may suppose, it is on the way to achieving.*
>
> *This aspect of Beethoven's work reverberates also in the expression of his death mask, which is beyond the borderline of empathy.*

Beethoven's great predecessor, the very young Mozart, wrote to his father, in 1787, when he heard of his father's last illness:

Since death (properly understood) is the true ultimate purpose of our life, I have for several years past made myself acquainted with this truest and best friend of mankind so that he has for me not only nothing terrifying anymore but much that is tranquillizing and consoling!

Jump a few centuries and hear what one of the world's great physicists, Albert Einstein, wrote to the son and sister of his lifelong friend Besso, who died exactly thirty-four days before Einstein himself succumbed: ". . . Now he's gone slightly ahead of me again, leaving this strange world. That doesn't mean anything. For us believing physicists this separation between past present and future has the value of mere illusion, however tenacious."

At a time when astronomers report that stars and quasars are "waltzing in space," who can doubt him?

Listen too to the eminent theologian Paul Tillich, when he spoke to the New York Academy of Sciences not long before his death:

If death is accepted by us already, we need not wait for it, be it near or far, with fear or with contempt. We know what it is because we have accepted. . . . We know it is the confirmation that we are creatures and that our end belongs to us. . . . In this way the riddle of life and death has ceased to be a riddle of thought or imagination; it has become a matter of life, here and now.

No one now writing has come closer to this riddle and this resolution than Alexander Solzhenitsyn in *Cancer Ward*.

This autumn [Kostoglotov says], *I learned from*

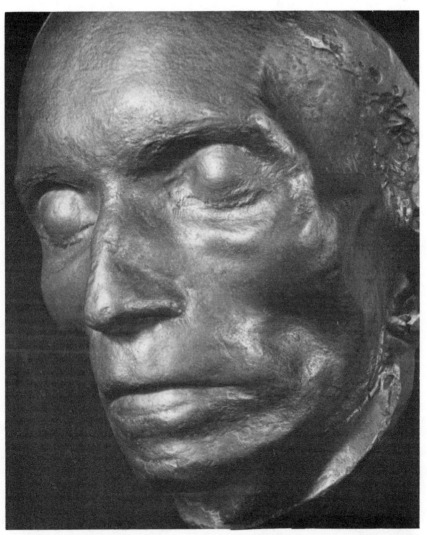

photo credit: Trude Fleischmann

Ludwig van Beethoven
1770–1827

Felix Mendelssohn-Bartholdy
1809–1847

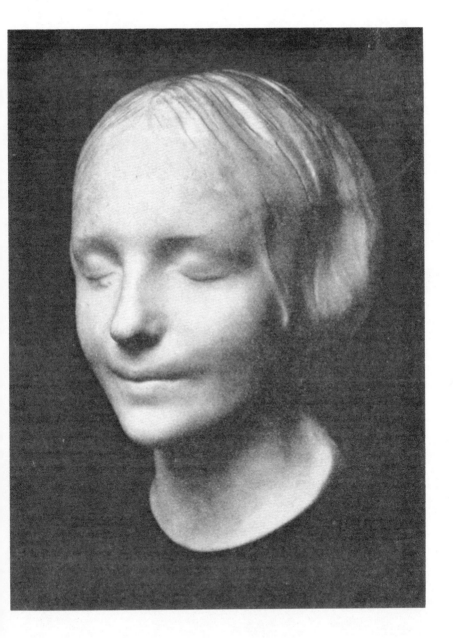

Unknown girl found in the Seine

Blaise Pascal
1623–1662

*experience that a man can cross the threshold
of death even when his body is still not dead.
Your blood still circulates and your stomach di-
gests, while you yourself have gone through the
whole psychological preparation for death—and
lived through death itself. Everything around
you, you see as if from the grave. And although
you've never counted yourself a Christian, indeed the very opposite sometimes, all of a sud-
den you find you've forgiven all those who
trespassed against you and bear no ill-will toward those who persecuted you. You're simply
indifferent to everyone and everything. There's
nothing you'd put yourself out to change, you
regret nothing. I'd even say it was a state of
equilibrium, as natural as that of the trees and
the stones. Now I have been taken out of it, but
I'm not sure whether I should be pleased or not.
It means the return of all my passions, the bad
as well as the good.*

One of Kostoglotov's negative (positive?) passions
is for the freedom of choice as to life or death denied
him by the medical-political bureaucracy and its hospital servants:

*Dontsova looked down at his colorless, wind-
ing scar and was silent. Kostoglotov developed
his point:*

*"You see, you start from a completely false
position. No sooner does a patient come to you
than you begin to do all his thinking for him.
After that, the thinking's done by your standing
orders, your five-minute conferences, your program, your plan and the honor of your medical
department. And once again I become a grain*

*of sand, just as I was in the camp. Once again
nothing* depends *on me."*

A great creative American spirit echoed this cry. In
his book on Eleanor Roosevelt's last years alone, Joseph
Lash writes that "There was only suffering for Mrs.
Roosevelt from the first day in July when she was taken
to the hospital for the first time. There was no moment
of serenity. There was only anger, helpless anger at the
doctors and nurses and the world who tried to keep her
alive. The doctors had her where they wanted her.

" 'They can do with me what they want, not what I
want,' she said bitterly."

Yet "she was not afraid of death at all. She welcomed
it. She was so weary and so infinitely exhausted, it
seemed as though she had to suffer every human indignity, every weakness, every failure that she had resisted and conquered so daringly during her whole
life—as though she were being punished for being too
strong and powerful and disciplined and almost im-
mune to human frailty."

And her punishment in a "free" society—so profoundly different from Kostoglotov's virtual prison—was
the same: impotence to exert her last human choice.

Some years earlier, Mrs. Roosevelt said on Edward R.
Murrow's "This I Believe":

> *I don't know whether I believe in a future life
> [but] I believe that all that you go through here
> must have some value, therefore there must be
> some* reason. *And there must be some "going
> on." How exactly that happens I've never been
> able to decide. There is a future—that I'm sure
> of. But how, that I don't know. And I came to
> feel that it didn't really matter very much be-
> cause whatever the future held you'd have to*

face it when you came to it, just as whatever life holds you have to face it in exactly the same way. And the important thing was that you never let down doing the best that you were able to do—it might be poor because you might not have much within you to give, or to help other people with, or to live your life with. But as long as you did the very best that you were able to do, then that was what you were put here to do and that was what you were accomplishing by being here.

" 'Not all of me shall die,' " whispered Shulubin, another patient in Solzhenitsyn's *Cancer Ward*, quoting Pushkin. " 'Not all of me shall die.'

Kostoglotov groped for the man's hot hand lying on the blanket. He pressed it lightly. "Aleksei Filippovich," he said, "you're going to live! Hang on, Aleksei Filippovich!"

"There's a fragment, isn't there? . . . Just a tiny fragment," he kept whispering.

It was then it struck Oleg that Shulubin was not delirious, that he'd recognized him and was reminding him of their last conversation before the operation. He had said, "Sometimes I feel quite distinctly that what is inside me is not all of me. There's something else, sublime, quite indestructible, some tiny fragment of the universal spirit. Don't you feel that?"

The great creators through time have not only felt it, but, through the relentless passion of their talents, been able to express it. Sublime or divine, often but by no means always impelled by religious faith, testaments to the "universal spirit" have defied time and death.

Whether they are Bach's *B Minor Mass* or Michelangelo's *Creation* or the *Winged Victory* or Shakespeare sonnets or Khmer heads or Christ's Sermon on the Mount or the prehistoric paintings in caves—the list is prodigious in origin, place, and time—the "tiny fragment" that no one can define still defies extinction, is indestructible.

It is also the product of human consciousness and human choice.

> *Eternity will be*
> *Velocity or pause,*
> *Precisely as the candidate*
> *Preliminary was.*

Emily Dickinson

XIII
The Alternatives

It is clear that not all of us are brave enough or able, when the end of life is actually close, to persist in demanding help to die or in taking whatever steps are available to leave this life with dispatch and dignity.

Religious scruples are not the only barriers to euthanasia. In fact, faith in God should bring with it belief in immortality, and sometimes does. The prayers of priests seem to lighten many souls in expiring bodies, assisting that "fair and easy passage."

Social and personal codes of morality and ethics make suicide for many unthinkable, even if the magnitude of the decision to kill oneself or help another to die were not in itself so daunting.

The independent spirit is still the rare one. The majority of us fear single action, and the responsibility for taking it is for most too heavy a burden. It is easier to do what others do; think what others think. Americans as a whole—like other peoples—are not the rugged individualists we used to call ourselves.

So although the movement for euthanasia is steadily growing, drawing more and more people into its ranks, becoming one of the major issues of humanity, alternate avenues must be kept open for those who cannot, or will not, bring themselves to join it.

After leaving the hospital, the choice for chronically ill or fragile old is sharply limited: return to home, in those dwindling instances when this is still possible for the family involved in their care; or the rest of life in an institution. Good or bad, this is at the very least a diminishment of self at mounting cost to the family, and at the worst a hell-hole of neglect and indifference; of existence at the lowest possible level.

In the good nursing homes, some can spend comparatively peaceful years, sustained by the company of their kind, solicitous care, hobbies for their distraction, and, of course, TV.

Of these, the small rural home, maintaining an atmosphere of consistent affection and human contact, seems the more preferable. Even the weakest and oldest can sit in the sun and watch living things and moving clouds and growing plants instead of venturing—if they are strong enough—on barren city streets, past relentless human and vehicular traffic.

Best of all, perhaps, is the kind of safe harbor represented by Youville, a Roman Catholic Hospital in Cambridge, Massachusetts. It is one of the seventy out of seven thousand private hospitals in this country that specializes in long-term rehabilitative and chronically ill patients, and has for the last four years pioneered in its program for counseling dying patients.

"We came to realize," said Youville's administrator Sister Annette Caron to a *New York Times* reporter, "that while we concentrated on the physical and medical care of the patients . . . we had missed their spiritual needs. . . . We came to the conclusion that, when a person is dying, you should not withdraw services from the patient—which is usually what happens—but you should do more to help him be a part of life as long as he is with us."

The staff psychiatrist at Youville, the Reverend Ned H. Cassem, has directed a program in conjunction with the Boston Theological Institute in which divinity students from seven graduate schools in the area come to the hospital weekly to visit with patients, and, above all, to listen to them.

The secret, Reverend Cassem says, is for the caretakers to learn from the dying and to respond to their needs as a vital antidote to the isolation normally imposed on them.

"The greatest fear the dying have," he concluded, "is the fear of dying alone, and that is a fear we can treat."

Of the many letters received at Youville, the following one, from the wife of a young man who had just died, was typical: "The importance to him was not so much to know that he would be mourned after he died, but the reality of knowing that he was loved while he lived. Speaking freely of death allowed us to taste more fully of life; those are the lessons the dying teach us."

On a much smaller scale, but imbued with the same spirit, is Calvary Hospital in the northern reaches of Manhattan island.

It looks like a model seminary of more stable years; red brick, white trimmed, three-storied, rising on a shoulder of rock and trees from the faceless streets of the Bronx. A green enclave, benign and peaceful.

And indeed it was a school until Calvary Hospital moved in 1914 from lower Manhattan to the abandoned school building ten or so miles to the north.

Yet as you walk up the winding concrete path and

the steps that lead to its entrance, you brace yourself for what you might see or hear. For Calvary is the end of the line: the place where the indigent, dying of cancer, are sent when the doctors are through with them.

Once inside, however, the sense of peace and light and—very palpably—love, is pervasive. You cross the immaculate and non-institutional foyer to the reception desk and ask for Miss Flannery, one of the guiding spirits, with Sister Gemma, of this retreat.

Knowing that it was founded over seventy years ago by a group of Catholic women, and came under the jurisdiction of the New York Archdiocese and the Dominican Sisters of the Sick Poor in 1958, you expect liturgical figurines and an aura of piety. Instead there are flowers and the patterns of branches outside the windows.

Soon, a young and extremely attractive woman in street clothes comes to you and takes you to her office upstairs. "I was a religious," said Miss Flannery, "and came here as a nun after getting my degree in social work from Fordham University." And then she told about Calvary.

"We have only a hundred and ten beds here to take in all the patients that nobody else wants. Mostly the poor on Medicaid, minority groups of all races and creeds.

"Many of them are referred here by Memorial Hospital—they are affiliated with us, and can't keep terminal cases. Some come from dreadful nursing homes, with maggots in their wounds from dirt and neglect. It is horrible what they do to defenseless people."

Miss Flannery told how the families who brought their relatives to Calvary broke down and wept at the cleanliness and concern. A great many of the patients had never been called Mr. or Mrs. before, or been spoken to gently as separate human beings.

Calvary has one nurse to three patients, she said, and a wonderful group of young volunteers. As we went through the corridors and visited a few of the wards, one could see the girls bending over and talking to the old, or—more importantly, said Miss Flannery—listening to them.

The two wards, with eight beds each, the rooms with two, were immaculate and bright. The old and very ill ranged, as usual, from immobile serenity—eyes opened, faces stripped of flesh to purified and often beautiful bone—to the foetal cramp of total negation or, quite apposite, to a bright still awareness of life in glance and movement.

"Most aren't told they have cancer," said Miss Flannery, "but they usually know." Very few despair, she said, but the poor black patients are the most resigned, partly because their whole lives have been resignation, endured only through faith in God. This was a mark of the older blacks, we agreed, and largely absent in the new generations.

Although about 15 percent of Calvary patients responded to treatment—the hospital had equipment for chemotherapy—and were able to return home, the average stay of most was thirty-four days until death. Not all were very old. Only yesterday, a young woman artist there had asked a volunteer to teach her how to pray.

Part of the active therapy treatment at Calvary took place in a room downstairs. There about fourteen elderly patients, mostly women and all in normal dress, sat around various tables making all sorts of things as they chatted, or worked in silence. Some were braiding or knitting, several created elaborate, gay and highly decorative boxes made of rice-grains and small shells or beads. A social worker gave help when they asked for it, supplied them with tools, material, or a guiding hand when the working hand faltered.

At a separate table a very thin black patient was building a wooden bird-house while a pretty Puerto Rican volunteer sat by, helping and joking. Apparently, it was hard to make contact with him—he was so withdrawn—so they took extra pains to bring him out. He was smiling now.

Apart from the arts and crafts program, Calvary provides occasional concerts and movies, and two barbecues a year for the patients and their families.

As in all hospitals, television was ubiquitous. "They love the daytime serials," said Miss Flannery. "They hate to miss a day." The ongoing story, perhaps, where there is always tomorrow?

There was no smell of death in this place where it claimed so many, so soon. Only compassion, and recognition long withheld.

"Working with the dying," said Miss Flannery, "can re-establish your own priorities."

Outstanding as Youville and Calvary and similar ports of last call may be, they are still primarily hospitals, not homes. That is why a remarkable place on the outskirts of London, St. Christopher's Hospice, is by wide agreement considered the best environment so far devised for life near its end.

Created and run by an equally remarkable woman, Dr. Cicely Saunders ("when she enters a room she fills it with light and warmth," said a visitor), it is exactly what its name implies: a house, a refuge, and a way station for travelers.

It is also a home, a family, and a community: staff and residents, relatives, listening, and touching, maintaining human contact whenever contact is wanted. Children, especially, are welcomed as a vital element of hospice life.

Among the many striking differences between St. Christopher's and even the most supportive nursing homes elsewhere is the emphasis on the basic need and pleasure of feeding, of which alcohol and heroin are regular elements.

The guests can have drinks at every evening meal . . . a choice of beer, wine, or hard liquor. The staff groups have sherry at their frequent gatherings and celebrations, and Dr. Saunders has been seen taking a bottle with her to visit a patient.

Alcohol is conceived here not as an indulgence but as a psychological, physiological, and social support.

As to the feeding of morphine and diamorphine, the staff is expert at eliminating pain, used in low and frequent doses to anticipate rather than alleviate suffering. The basic drug, however, is heroin. Although it induces euphoria, the staff knows that patients in pain are far below their natural level of well-being, and that the drug merely raises it to a normal threshold.

When death does come, the dying are never alone. An American volunteer chaplain serving at St. Christopher's said, "I discovered . . . that watching with the dying becomes, eventually, a welcoming of death."

Since his experience, more and more visitors confirm not only his enthusiasm but the conviction that the hospice concept is one that we should adopt forthwith for the pressing, largely unanswered needs of our own aged and dying. Already, one modeled largely on the English prototype and spearheaded by Miss Florence Wald, a registered nurse, is being built in New Haven; and euthanasia supporters are now giving highest priority to the ultimate plan of having others rise in every community.

The funds needed for this wide-scale planning are of course great, not only in terms of the buildings themselves but in the numbers and quality of the needed staff. As everyone knows, and one look at New York City confirms, it costs more to build a small edifice for basic and urgent human needs than to raise a huge monolith for commercial profit.

Yet the enormous amount of space involved in big hospital complexes for the old and chronically ill and the corresponding enormities of medical costs must certainly far exceed those, in any community, of creating and running a hospice. Even doctors, among our most affluent citizens, would find this hard to refute. They might even welcome the added space in hospitals freed for the nonterminal patient. Their objection might concern itself more with the absence of those miraculous machines which, in the prolonging of organic existence, conveniently come between themselves and the dying, relieving them from that touching and speaking so vital to people near death.

Yet even if the hospice concept is accepted as valid and needed, it may well take years until the existence of many across this nation becomes a reality.

For that long time till then, the only hope for a "good and gentle death," for dying in dignity, remains in the education of society itself, and of those who order its patterns: the state, the Church, the law, and medicine.

It also remains in the individual conscience and courage of those who insist on this dignity. Those who refuse to end their lives with addled brains or punctured bodies strung to life substitutes—they must not make this refusal clear only to themselves. They must sign the forms now available at the euthanasia centers, they must make their choice known in writing at regular stated intervals to their lawyers and doctors as well as their kin, they must fight in their legislatures for the repeal of punitive laws making this easement of death and spirit a legal offense. (Again, the legislating of morality seldom achieves it. It only invades the constitutional right of privacy.)

Brave or not, it is imperative for this adult generation to make death a matter of life to their children. It is more than possible that their whole concept of dying has been warped either by the silence surrounding it, the attitudes of their family, or the chronic dosage of death by violence on television and movies. Where is the dignity in the riddled body, the bloodied corpse, the broken neck?—deaths without meaning or reality to them, like the limp corpses of soldiers sprawled on a blasted and distant field.

The young might also learn as much about life as about death if their parents showed them this passage by the remarkable young German poet Rainer Maria Rilke, writing in the early nineteen hundreds to a depressed older friend:

> *We must assume our existence as broadly as we in any way can; everything, even the unheard-of, must be possible in it. That is at bottom the only courage that is demanded of us: to have courage for the most extraordinary, the most singular and the most inexplicable that we may encounter. That mankind has in this sense been cowardly has done life endless harm; the experiences that are called "appearances," the*

so-called "spirit-world," death, all those things that are so closely akin to us, have by daily parrying been so driven out of life that the senses with which we could have grasped them are crippled.

XIV
Where Are We Now?

Last year, over fifty thousand Americans wrote to the Euthanasia Educational Fund in New York for free copies of "A Living Will," and since then the requests have multiplied steadily. The "will" is a short testament addressed to a patient's family, physician, clergyman, and lawyer. It says in part, "If there is no reasonable expectation of my recovery from physical or mental disability, I request that I be allowed to die and not be kept alive by artificial means or heroic measures.

"I do not fear death," the document continues, "as much as I fear the indignity of deterioration, dependence, and hopeless pain. I ask that drugs be mercifully administered to me for terminal suffering even if they hasten the moment of death."

The Living Will has no legal weight, but the addressees can seldom ignore it with conscience.

Whatever their ultimate outcome, and so far no action has been taken, bills are being proposed in a few state legislatures, of which the following is a superior example:

It was proposed in New York State by a committee of 1,776 physicians who want legislation to make euthanasia lawful, so that they and their patients may be protected from possible prosecution for a practice which, as everyone knows, goes on anyway. The bill is backed by the Euthanasia Society of America, and by thousands of doctors. It provides three things, essentially: "(1) any sane person over twenty-one years old, suffering from an incurably painful and fatal disease, may petition a court of record for euthanasia, in a signed and attested document, with an affidavit from the attending physician that in his opinion the disease is incurable; (2) the court shall appoint a commission of three, of whom at least two shall be physicians, to investigate all aspects of the case and to report back to the courts whether the patient understands the purpose of his petition and comes under the provisions of the act; (3) upon a favorable report by the commission the court shall grant the petition, and *if it is still wanted by the patient* euthanasia may be administered by a physician or any other person chosen by the patient or by the commission."

A euthanasia bill is pending in the Hawaii Legislature, and the Montana Constitutional Convention has been urged to "allow every citizen to choose the manner in which he dies."

A column by Clayton Fritchey in the *New York Post* last year mentions Jerome Nathanson, chairman of the New York Society for Ethical Culture, as believing that the more open and honest ways of American youth will help advance acceptance of euthanasia. Nathanson, whose wife died of cancer, spoke of a doctor attending a terminal patient who leaves three pills on the bedside table saying, "Take one every four hours. If you take them all at once, they will kill you." Doctors are well aware of this approach even when they deny their use of it.

Dr. Joseph Fletcher, professor of ethics at Episcopal Theological School in Cambridge, said, "Indirect euthanasia is being practiced in thousands and thousands of cases involving terminal illnesses."

Courses in death are becoming increasingly popular on secular as well as theological campuses, and clergymen in increasing numbers have been joining seminars on the terminally ill. In a report on this recent development, *The New York Times* wrote that "they have not abandoned their role of bringing spiritual comfort. But many have been trying to listen more and to speak of faith only when it is appropriate." And about a dozen major seminaries have instituted courses on dying which often "emphasize psychology more than religion."

Articles on death and dying have been appearing with increasing regularity in the major newspapers and magazines, inspiring, to be sure, the expected and often angry reactions of which this letter to *The New York*

Times is typical. Among other objections to an editorial called "Death With Dignity," Reverend G. V. Haddock writes:

> *If you do believe in God, perhaps you will also grant that suffering could be part of God's plan for man's purification—we certainly are faced with quite a bit of it—since we are all sinners and need the opportunity to make amends for our misdeeds.*
>
> *A man who believes in God and acts according to God's dictates need be afraid neither of death itself, whenever God's providence decrees it, nor of a long period of illness, even of the type you describe as "calamitous" or "emotionally and financially draining."*

———————

Last year, two network programs dared in prime time to devote an hour each to the dread five-letter word and explore the time before dying. "The Bold Ones" on ABC not only prefaced its drama, called "An Absence of Loneliness," by saying "The most significant fact of life is Death," but explored the struggle of six dying patients to communicate—to wife, son, nurse, or doctor—in their different and separate ways the essence of what they were going through.

Some of these relationships were tinged with theatricality, but there was one small scene of an elderly terminal patient that went to the core of the matter. She was complaining to her doctor that her nurse kept offering her fruit juice when what she so desperately needed instead was attention. "No one pays *attention!*" she cried. If it accomplished nothing else, the play bore home the crucial need of talk: the acknowledgment of all concerned that only by facing death squarely and fearlessly can the dread dissipate or be transformed into acceptance and peace.

Even "Marcus Welby, M.D." tried to come to grips with dying in "A Necessary End." The terminal patient is a famous photographer, played by Anne Baxter, whose life is her camera. Although she is supposed to be the victim of fatal cardiac complications (the doctor bravely tells her so), she shows neither pain nor erosion, fluttering her false eyelashes happily when Welby suggests that she must keep on snapping till the end. Why not take photographs of other celebrities at the end of *their* span? This she does, surrounding herself with the terminal (and adoring) great, and looking lovely till (confessing wistfully that her life had never been full because she had not been wife or mother) she keels over—dead.

Not long before this soap fable, and in sharp contrast, Public Television showed a BBC documentary that concerned a young sculptor: the victim of a serious car accident that ruptured his spinal cord and paralyzed his arms, among other injuries. In the hospital, the dialogue contains the following exchanges:

> PATIENT (*to doctor*): You only grow vegetables here. . . . I prefer not to take drugs. I've decided not to stay alive.
> DOCTOR: Because you're depressed?
> PATIENT: Sculpting . . . with no hands? I am serious about deciding to die. I do not choose to be happy by being part of a complex machine. (*To his lawyer*) Get me out of here . . . I want to be discharged to die. Present my views to the doctor.

LAWYER (*to doctor*): Mr. Harris wants to die.
. . . He must be discharged from the hospital.
DOCTOR: It's impossible. . . . Mr. Harris is mentally unbalanced.
PATIENT: It is *my* decision.
LAWYER: I'll take it to court on habeas corpus.
DOCTOR: Mr. Harris is suffering from a mental depression.
PATIENT: I wish to die. I'm dead already. You're keeping my brain active without any activity or decision. It's a question of dignity. I can't do any basic primitive functions. . . . Dignity is choice. If I choose to die the hospital is appalling to keep me alive.
LAWYER (*to doctor*): Mr. Harris is a cool and courageous man.

Last spring, Plays for Living (a division of the Family Service Association of America), which brings half-hour original dramas on vital subjects to over two hundred cities in this country, came to grips with death.

Called "You Didn't Know My Father" and acted by five professional actors, with no scenery or props except chairs, the entire dialogue took place in the waiting room of an intensive-care unit of a hospital.

It mirrored the agonies of conflict in the relatives of three dying patients kept "alive" by machines. Two wanted all measures taken and hope sustained. One—the grown son of an adored father—did not. Remembering him as the splendid man of force and dignity he once was, but now felled by three strokes, unconscious and helpless, the son wanted to "let him go."

Intensely poignant, honest, and compassionate, the play has been performed before high-school audiences, civic groups, and professional organizations across the nation.

———

These, with many other unrecorded examples, are straws in a wind that blows more strongly every day, scattering dead leaves of old attitudes, clearing the air, the mind, and the spirit.

It is neither a frightening wind nor a destructive one. It should bring to the old and to all who value life a sense of clarification and release. "We have met the enemy and he is not an enemy." No longer the pawns of doctrines or machines, well-meaning relatives or medical technology, we shall not be powerless. If we cannot determine our birth, we will at least be able to determine the conditions of our dying.

It is even possible that death is an opening as well as a closing. We shall at the very least continue to live in those whom we loved and who love us.

And we shall be part of an orchestration conceived by a humane vision and not by an arbitrary power.

Death in the right circumstances is both right and our right. If we have lived to the fullest of our capacities, dying is merely suspension within a mystery. If our lives have seemed wasted or futile, death is more reprieve than reprimand.

Believing this, we should not be intimidated or thwarted by the counterarguments of the state, the Church, the law, society, or medicine itself. We have heard them all, but the final choice must be ours.

This is why I now express my own terms in the matter

of life and death. It is meant to be neither a model nor an example. Yet if it gives direction and courage, it will have served its purpose.

To: My Doctor—
My Lawyer—
My Closest Relative—
My Dear Friend—

I ask each of you, in concert or individually, to assure that certain measures be taken to end my life should I fall victim to the following circumstances. Singly or together, they would deprive me of all that I cherish most in living, preferring death to their loss. *

1. Any disease or accident that would leave me unable to take care of my own bodily functions or deprive me of independent mobility.

2. Progressive deterioration of mind as evinced by total loss of memory, only partial consciousness, chronically irrational behavior, delirium, or any other evidence of advanced senility.

3. Any condition requiring the use—beyond two weeks—of mechanical equipment for breathing, heart action, feeding, dialysis, or brain function without a prognosis of full recovery of my vital organs.

4. Any progressive deterioration of muscle, bone, or tissue requiring an increasing dependence on intravenous substances, and without realistic hope for recovery consistent with my definition of such.

---

* Note: This document to be re-signed by me every two years up to and until the event that loss of consciousness through accident or illness precludes my signature. In this case, the wishes expressed are to be carried out by the person herein addressed.

5. I do not wish to survive a stroke that impairs my ability to speak or move, nor any accident or disease resulting in vision too impaired to see or read, or in total deafness.

A world without beauty heard or seen is no world for me.

A life without freedom and movement is no life for me.

If age and illness deny me these, I choose death. And if a difference of opinion among you results in ignoring or only partially acceding to these requests, then I beg that one of you provide me with the means to take my own life while in a conscious state.

XV
Transcendence

Once Ilych was alone and in his final throes, Tolstoy describes him as feeling that "In place of death, there was light. . . .

" 'So that's what it is!' he suddenly exclaimed aloud. 'What joy!'. . . ."
And then, when he heard someone say, "It is finished," he said, in his soul, "Death is finished."

———

"We must assume our existence as *broadly* as we in any way can; everything, even the unheard-of, must be possible in it." None could have agreed with Rilke more than a group of researchers working at a little-known project at the Maryland Psychiatric Center at Catonsville, outside Baltimore.

The reason why they are not publicized is that they have been working for several years on the use of LSD and other psychedelic drugs as psychic supports in therapy for the dying. Since they are dealing with drugs proscribed by law to the general population and allowed by the government only in limited and strictly supervised quantities, their work is slow, and their volunteer patients—seriously and terminally ill—a small sample for what seems to qualified observers an extremely important advance.

One of these observers, a fourth-year student at the Harvard Medical School and a writer, Jerry Avorn, spent time at Catonsville and reported what he saw, prefacing his account with the remark that "Western civilization has steadily narrowed its view of the broad spectrum of consciousness, focusing on the pure cool light of science to the exclusion of the more subtle and exotic colors beyond. Rationality has given us. . . . laser-guided missiles, and electric can-openers in exchange for the kingdom within."

Transcripts show that a new "kingdom within" has become manifest in some of the patients at Catonsville through a combination of exalted music (*Death and Transfiguration*, the climax of *Tristan and Isolde*, and Gounod's *St. Cecilia Mass* were among those mentioned as typical), LSD, psychotherapy, and eyeshades to diminish distraction. Throughout their treatment, a therapist is at their bedside.

One fifty-year-old patient described the first part of her "trip" as being "part of everything filthy and ugly," traveling down a steadily narrowing black tunnel of gloom and misery, seeing a vulture that she took as Death or the Devil (shades of Hieronymus Bosch?), and "when I forced myself to look at the end [of the tunnel], I found whatever it was I was afraid to look at was *nothing*. . . .

"After seeing all these horrible things, I came up to the beautiful and wonderful. I continued to go higher,

passing among billions . . . of minute spirits like my-
self. I felt a very, very small part of the whole thing.
There seemed a small place above and beyond every-
thing else, and I found myself being drawn to this place.
After getting to this peak, I found who I thought was
God. . . ."

The "bad trip" of this general pattern could be inter-
preted as the final divesting of all that was ugly and
contaminated in the dying flesh so that the spirit could
break through to some ultimate purity: not always
translated into terms of God or Jesus, but as belonging
to the universal whole.

. Dr. Grof, a Czech-born psychiatrist who had pioneered in LSD therapy, suggested that the idea of possible continuity of consciousness beyond physical death
becomes much more plausible than the opposite. The
patients develop a rather deep belief in the cosmic unity
of all creation and experience.

A novel written by myself in 1947 concerned the
diary of a woman who had died and who retained her
consciousness of earth only when those she knew and
loved were thinking of her. (The flyleaf of *Message
From a Stranger* quoted Joseph Conrad: "The dead can
live only with the exact intensity and quality of life
imparted to them.")

It is mentioned here because the heroine's description
of her death astonishingly parallels Grof's words thirty-
five years later. "Then it happened. I remember one
final spasm, not unlike the birth of Philip. And I remember thinking to myself, this must be the delivery of my
soul; and I saw then a primitive Italian painting in reds
and blues where, from the prostrated body of a noble
lord, escapes the white puff of his spirit, freed. But there
was a strange addition: I was for a time both the bearer
and the borne, the issuant and the issue. I was at the

same moment creating and being created, and I could not tell which was the more arduous: the black hot fighting up into light, or the more familiar expulsion of my burden. . . .

"First, with a fearful roar and clanging, as if a thousand metal hearts were beating against their walls, I was whirled into an emptiness as crowded with a substance as are certain silences with sound. It was a wild and headlong flight, where I spun and reeled and palpitated like a leaf in a hurricane. In all this roaring and palpitation there was music—phrases, voices, instruments engaged in some gigantic cosmic tuning up; a perpetual prelude—to what symphony . . . ?

"The headlong rush . . . then stopped, and a great silence came. I seemed to be quivering like a seismographic needle; suspended in a stationary dance as a part of some microscopic palpitation. This dance took place in an electric and impalpable space that had no boundaries. . . .

"I was not alone. In this featureless state there was a definite pattern, of which I was only one point of many. I remember once seeing a 'model' of an atom—several white balls jiggling and palpitating around a central ball. This, presumably, was the final breakdown of matter.

"A great peace settled over me. I had not realized until this moment how heavy was the burden of identity."

I know now that the burden of lost identity, as in the trapped and helpless and dying, is even worse.

That is why I wrote this book. To try to help free them, to transcend death.

Epilogue

"A last duty. Human life consists in mutual service. No grief, no pain, no misfortune or 'broken heart' is excuse for cutting off one's life while any power of service remains. But when all usefulness is over, when one is assured of an imminent and unavoidable death, it is the simplest of human rights to choose a quick and easy death in place of a slow and horrible one. Public opinion is changing on this subject. The time is approaching when we shall consider it abhorrent to our civilization to allow a human being to lie in prolonged agony which we should mercifully end in any other creature. Believing this choice to be of social service in promoting wider views on this question, I have preferred chloroform to cancer."

Last words, typed by herself, of
Charlotte Perkins Gilman

Source: Quote by A. L. Woolbarst,
Medical Record, May 17, 1939.

Bibliography

Eissler, K. R., *The Psychiatrist and the Dying Patient.* New York, International Universities Press, 1955.

Fletcher, Joseph, *Morals and Medicine.* Boston, Beacon Press (Paperback), 1960.

Garnett, Richard, "Jonathan Swift" in *Encyc. Brit.*, 11th ed.

Hendin, David, *Death as a Fact of Life.* New York, Norton, 1973.

Kübler-Ross, Elisabeth, *On Death and Dying.* New York, Macmillan, 1969.

Lash, Joseph P., *Eleanor: The Years Alone.* New York, Norton, 1972.

Ramsey, Paul, *The Patient as Person.* New Haven, Yale University Press, 1970.

Rilke, Rainer Maria, *Letters to a Young Poet.* New York, Norton, 1934.

Russell, Bertrand, *Why I Am Not a Christian.* New York, Simon and Schuster, 1957.

Schoenberg, Bernard, and others, *Psychosocial Aspects*

of Terminal Care. New York, Columbia University Press, 1972.

Schur, Max, *Freud Living and Dying*. New York, International Universities Press, 1972.

Solzhenitsyn, Alexander, *Cancer Ward*. New York, Bantam (Paperback), 1969.

Strauss, Anselm L. and Glaser, Barney G., *Anguish*. Mill Valley, Calif., Sociology Press, 1970.

Sullivan, J. W. N., *Beethoven*. New York, Mentor (Paperback), 1949.

Tolstoy, Leo, *The Death of Ivan Ilych and Other Stories*. New York, New American Library (Paperback), 1960.

Weisman, Avery D., *On Dying and Denying*. New York, Behavioral Publications, 1972.

White, Laurens P., ed., *Care of Patients with Fatal Illness*. Annals of the New York Academy of Sciences, Vol. 164, Art. 3. New York, December 19, 1969.

Winter, Arthur, ed., *The Moment of Death*, a symposium. Springfield, Ill., Charles C. Thomas, 1969.

Index